WORLD WAR 1

AMERICA AND THE GREAT WAR

A 100TH ANNIVERSARY

ILLUSTRATED COMMEMORATIVE

BY

PHILIP A. KEITH

SECOND EDITION

D1418013

Table of Contents

⊙ Author's Introduction

Cpl. Frank Buckles,1918   Frank Buckles-2007

When Frank Buckles died, on February 27, 2011, at the age of 110, the final living link between the United States and the Great War was severed. His eyes were the last to have gazed upon the Western Front for America. He was the last to experience the war as it was, in all of its terrifying magnificence. He was the end of a very long line.

Following the Congressional Declaration that catapulted the United States—belatedly—into the Great War, on April 6, 1917, America quickly registered an astonishing 4,355,000 men as eligible to serve. The War Department mobilized over two million of the able–bodied registrants and volunteers, turned them into "Doughboys," and sent half of them overseas in less than eighteen months.[1] By the end of the war, on November 11, 1918, America was shipping 10,000 troops a day to France. After the last guns fell silent, and the "butcher's bill" was totaled, 116,516 of Frank Buckles comrades in arms were dead and another 204,002 were wounded. Of the Americans sent to fight, the overall casualty rate was a shade over seven percent. This was a pittance compared to the 70% casualty rates of Russia, France, and Romania and Austria-Hungary's staggering 90%. Nonetheless, every death and every wounding affected a relative, family member, or friend back home in the States.

The war had a profound effect, and not just on its participants. The echoes from that war kept reverberating and they were still fresh in the minds of many when a second worldwide war broke out a scant twenty-one years later.

Many excellent books have been written on the causes and effects of what was then called the Great War—the "war to end all wars;" which, of course it wasn't. This book is not in that vein: what I have sought to do herein, as a narrator-author, is to commemorate the war through strictly American eyes, like those of Frank Buckles. This is a documentary, in literary form, of the uniquely American experiences between 1914, when the Great War exploded across Europe, and 1917,

---

[1] Women were not subject to registration or conscription, but approximately 35,000 served, most as nurses.

when America finally joined the fighting. We will also look at the Yanks in the war, how they fared, and what happened to them immediately after they came home.

One hundred years ago America embarked on her first great adventure in global conflict and world-wide politics. Nothing has been the same since.

Phil Keith
Southampton, NY
2019

⊙ 1914: "The True Spirit of Neutrality"

A snapshot taken of America as the Great War[2] commenced, in July, 1914, would have revealed these statistics: We were a nation about to cross the 100 million mark in total population and we lived in 48 contiguous states. Arizona and New Mexico had only joined the Union two years prior, and statehood for Alaska and Hawaii were decades into the future. Woodrow Wilson, a Democrat, was mid-way through his first term as President. Both houses of the 63rd Congress were also controlled by the Democratic Party.

An adult American male could expect to live to 52, on average, and women, faring better, could reasonably count on a span of 57 years. Equality among the sexes was being hotly debated because women still did not have the right to vote. Obtaining that right (called "women's suffrage") was becoming an important national cause.

Race relations between blacks and whites had gone from bad to worse: many of the reforms envisioned after the Civil War and Reconstruction had simply failed to materialize. In the South a series of "Jim Crow" laws unique to many of the ex-Confederate states were on the books. These measures were intended to keep African-Americans "in their place." As a result, with economic opportunities almost non-existent, a large

---

[2] It was not called "World War I" until World War II came along

population migration among blacks from south-to-north was underway.

There were already over a million and a half automobiles registered to drive on the two and a half million miles of roads stitched across America; but, there was not yet a way to drive across the country on a connected network of reliable highway surfaces. Thanks mostly to Henry Ford and his magical automobile assembly line, a complete Model-T could be manufactured in about ninety minutes and the cost to own one dropped to about $500.00. Ford Motor Company would crank out over a quarter million Model-T's in 1914.

Additionally, Mr. Ford paid his workers the astonishing wage of $5 per day which was equal to an entire week's pay for a skilled worker in Great Britain. Gasoline to run your Model-T was fifteen cents a gallon. Recognizing what was coming, the very first traffic light was installed in Cleveland, Ohio, at the intersection of Euclid and 105th Street, in August. A little further east, in New York City, the traffic cone was invented by Mr. Charles Rudabaker. They were made out of concrete, though, not the plastic types we are familiar with today.

The American office or industrial worker (who was, by far, male) earned, on average, $577 a year. Farmers made about $25.00 per month and produced a prodigious amount of product. Plumbers made sixty-nine cents an hour, carpenters sixty-five cents, painters fifty cents and bricklayers seventy-five cents. Milk was thirty-six cents a gallon, eggs thirty-five cents a dozen, loaves of bread six cents each, coffee was thirty cents a pound, and sirloin steaks were twenty-six cents a pound.

Newly invented items you could spend your 1914 income on included: Tinkertoys[3], Listerine mouthwash, and Tastycakes. You could snap your brand-new Wrigley's Doublemint gum as you did the latest dance, something called the foxtrot, and you could sing the year's number one new song, "It's a Long Way to Tipperary."

An average house cost $6,156.00; but, most homes did not yet have indoor plumbing. Domiciles were becoming electrified, however, and you could have a telephone, electric air conditioner, electric vacuum, electric washer, and an electric refrigerator—if not a flushing toilet.

The Bureau of Internal Revenue issued its very first tax form, the venerable 1040, which is still in use today, although a lot more complicated. The soon-to-be widely disliked IRS came into being after the 16th Amendment to the Constitution was ratified in 1913. The first income tax rate was very simple: one-percent on incomes above $3000 and a six percent surtax was imposed on income earned above $500,000.00.

---

[3] A construction set of round wheels and smooth sticks, all made of wood, used to fashion small machines and toys

America was on the periphery of massive change but the whole world spun away on a different trajectory when the fateful shots that killed Archduke Franz Ferdinand and his wife rang out in Sarajevo that June. It would take a while for the game changing events in Europe to reach the shores of America, but the die was being cast as the warm summer sun of 1914 baked the nation. Here are some of the other events that dominated life in the United States in 1914 as the Old World began to tear itself apart:

Major Events in America, 1914:

The year started on a high note, literally, as the very first airline passenger flight took off on New Year's Day. The St. Petersburg-Tampa Airboat Line began regular passenger service between those two Florida cities on January 1st. The inaugural airline passenger was the mayor of St. Petersburg and the first federally licensed airline pilot, Tony Janus, flew himself and the mayor in a two-seat flying boat twenty-one miles across Tampa Bay at an altitude of fifty feet. The trip took twenty-three minutes. The mayor paid $400 for his ticket, but that was only after a charity auction seeking the highest bidder. The regular passenger fare would be a much more modest $5.00.

January was also a pioneering month for the automobile business. On the 5th, Henry Ford introduced the concept of the eight hour workday and announced to a shocked world—including his own workers—that henceforth he would pay his people the eye-popping wage of $5.00 per day. This more than doubled the previous rate of pay for the auto workers and made them some of the highest paid semi-skilled workers in the world. Mr. Ford had another trick up his sleeve, too: on the 14th, he unveiled his first modern assembly line, an innovation that would forever change the automobile business and much of the manufacturing world as well.

On February 7th, British actor Charlie Chaplin (1889-1977) debuted his most famous role, that of "the Little Tramp," under contract to Keystone Studios. The mustachioed mischief maker in a bowler hat would become an endearing character in numerous silent movies until the "talkies" took over in the late 1920's.

February 12th, Abraham Lincoln's birthday, was a cold, sun-streaked day, but marked by the laying of the cornerstone of the famous Memorial that would rise to honor the former President. After many years of Congressional wrangling, an allocation had finally been passed budgeting $300,000 for the construction of the monument. Former President William Howard Taft was the head of the Lincoln Memorial Commission. Completion would take another eight years with a final dedication held on May 30, 1922. Lincoln's only surviving child, Robert Todd Lincoln (1843-1926), a former Secretary of War, was in attendance.

In March, birth control activist Margaret Sanger began publishing her feminist newspaper *Woman Rebel.* The masthead of the paper boldly declared: "No Gods No Masters." The US Postal Service took exception to using the mail for the paper's circulation and tried—unsuccessfully—to suppress its distribution. During the same month, Congress passed a law denying entry visas to known foreign socialists and anarchists.

April was a month fraught with contentious issues that brought discord at home and abroad. The so-called "Tampico Affair" erupted on the 9th: a group of US Navy sailors, ashore in Tampico, Mexico, seeking fuel for their ship, were mistaken for opposition forces by Mexican federal soldiers. Tensions nearly escalated to violence, but the un-armed Navy men were finally taken into custody and marched to the nearby Mexican regimental headquarters. Loyalties were eventually sorted out, and the US sailors released; but, the local US Navy commander, Rear Admiral Henry T. Mayo, demanded a formal apology from the government of Mexican President General Victoriano Huerta. He didn't get it.

In truth, relations between the two North American neighbors had been problematic, at best, since early 1913, when Huerta had wrestled control of the government away from its duly elected president. It didn't help that several days after the coup, the former president and vice president of Mexico were mysteriously murdered. From this point forward, Mexico plunged into years of revolution, something that would be of great concern to her powerful northern neighbor. Complicating matters was the government of Germany, headed by the bellicose Kaiser Wilhelm II, no friend of America. Germany had designs on Mexico; or, at the very least, using Mexico as a puppet to hector the United States. Naturally, this did not sit well with President Wilson.

Wilson immediately backed Admiral Mayo and sent additional Naval forces to Mexico, including several destroyers, battleships, torpedo ships, and a large contingent of US Marines. By April 22nd, Wilson was seeking support from the US Congress for movement against Huerta's regime. He got permission, but action was already underway: Two days earlier, Wilson had ordered the Navy to seize the Port of Veracruz. There was some urgency to get this done since Wilson knew, at the time, that a German freighter was entering the port loaded to the gunwales with arms and ammunition for the Huerta forces.

Heading the Naval invasion force was Mayo's boss, Rear Admiral Frank Friday Fletcher (1855-1928), an 1875 graduate of the US Naval Academy. During the morning of the 21st, Fletcher ordered his Marines and Bluejackets (armed Navy sailors) over the sides of their ships with orders to secure the Port of Veracruz. The one-thousand sailors and marines met no opposition as they landed along the wharves. The men formed up into smart-looking groups and marched off to secure their objectives which were, initially, all the docks and port facilities. The sailors were told to capture the post office, telegraph office, and the customs house. The Marines were directed to secure the power plant, the railroad terminal, and all the rail facilities.

The defense of Veracruz was spotty, at best. The Mexican commanding general had few troops at his disposal, so he began arming the civilian population. The Cadets at the Mexican Naval Academy were also pressed into service. The fighting went from house to house and street to street, growing more intense over the next two days. More Marines came ashore and the guns from the US Navy ships began to pound targets in the city. Finally, on the 24th, all resistance was overcome and Veracruz was secured. The dictator Huerta had been taught a lesson, American might had prevailed, and the offending cargo ship full of weapons was turned away (although it later landed at another port friendly to President Huerta).

The American forces lost twenty-two dead and seventy wounded. Mexican losses totaled between 152-172 military personnel killed and an unknown number of civilians dead and wounded. The Secretary of the Navy showered fifty-six Medals of Honor on the victorious Marines and Navy men, which turned out to be the largest number of awards of the Medal handed down for any single action before or since. One legendary

Marine, then-Major (later Major General) Smedley D. Butler, tried to refuse his Medal of Honor saying he had not done enough to deserve it. He was ordered not only to accept it, but to wear it. Admiral Fletcher was awarded a Medal of Honor for his handling of the whole affair; and, in a curious twist, so was his nephew, then-Lieutenant Frank "Jack" Fletcher, who would go on to even greater fame as one of the "Fighting Admirals" of WW II. Lieutenant Fletcher received his Medal of Honor in recognition of his having rescued over 350 refugees from the fighting at Veracruz.

The occupation of Veracruz continued for an additional six months until diplomacy finally ended America's involvement. All United States forces were out of Veracruz by November 23rd and both countries began trying to mend their political fences.

As if President Wilson wasn't having enough difficulty during April, 1914, there was more turmoil—this time at home. The scene was Ludlow, Colorado, near the Rocky Mountains, amidst the sprawling Colorado coal fields. The existence of plentiful reserves of coal close to the surface had been uncovered in 1867 by land surveyors from the Kansas Pacific Railway. By 1910, over 15,000 people were working the mines that sprang up. The largest of the mining companies was Colorado Fuel & Iron, owned by John D. Rockefeller. Conditions in these mines were, in a word, deplorable. In addition to the dirty and dangerous work, mine safety was largely ignored. The miners and their families lived in company-owned "coal towns" where their lives were strictly monitored. Company guards with loaded weapons patrolled the workforce, keeping the miners under control and at work. CF&I owned the homes, the shops, the grocery outlets, the medical facilities, and paid miners in company scrip, further chaining them to what was essentially a modern feudal system. Over 1,800 miners died on the job between the years 1884 and 1913.

The workers wanted better wages, safer conditions, better education for their children, and upgraded medical care. The Rockefellers were not interested in listening to their employees; so, as a consequence, the miners and their leaders sought out union representation. By mid-1913 the United Mine Workers of America (UMWA) had successfully infiltrated the mining workforce, secretly signing up thousands of members, and presented a list of demands for improved conditions and work rules to the owners. All the demands were rejected and the UMWA called a general strike in September, 1913.

The strikers were forced from their company homes, but the union had been prepared for that: it had leased parcels of land near the mine entrances and set up "tent cities" for the miners and their families. The mine owners responded by hiring a thuggish private detective agency to protect the strike-breaking new miners as well as harass the strikers.

The agent-detectives did all they could to break the strike, including using searchlights at night to disrupt sleep and firing random shots into the tents. Several were killed and wounded. The guards also fashioned an "armored car" out of steel plates and the body of a big sedan. The "Death Special" as it was called had a mounted machine gun and spent its time patrolling the camp perimeters, frightening and intimidating the strikers and their families.

As the strike dragged on, the governor of Colorado called out the National Guard. The Guard managed to restore some order, but the officers were, in general, sympathetic to the mine owners; so, the strikers were even more beset with woes. By early 1914, the strike had nearly collapsed, as the Guard and owners brought in more and more substitute ("scab") labor. The State, however, ran out of funds for the Guard, and had to recall all but one company of troops. The mine owners responded with forming their own, paid-for company of "Guardsmen" who were nothing more than former camp guards and thugs from the old private detective agency who donned Guard uniforms and continued on with their old harassment tactics.

It all came to a disastrous head on April 20th when two companies of Guardsmen descended on the Ludlow Camp and set up machine guns. The nervous miners responded by grabbing their personal weapons. It didn't take long for a rolling, day long gunfight to erupt. Four women and eleven children hid in a pit under one large tent. The Guardsmen set the tent on fire and all eleven children and two of the four women were burned to death. Three union leaders were captured and executed on the spot, and three guardsmen plus one militiaman perished.

News of the so-called "Ludlow Massacre" swept across Colorado like a prairie fire. Union members and miners throughout the coal fields took up arms. There were ten days of violence, shootings, destruction, and death. On the 28th, President Wilson, with great reluctance, sent in Federal troops, who quickly restored order, disarmed all the combatants, and ordered the Colorado National Guard out of the coalfields.

It was a watershed moment in American labor relations. Reforms started to fall into place: The Rockefeller family was so shaken that they hired a labor relations expert to help develop plans to improve conditions in the mines. The UMWA bought the Ludlow site in 1916 and by 1918 had erected a monument commemorating those who had died during the riots. The tent colony site was declared a US National Historic Landmark in 2009.

On a lighter note, President Wilson signed a Proclamation on May 7th declaring that the second Sunday in May, henceforth, would be a national holiday celebrating all mothers; thus, Mother's Day was initiated.

The ominous month of June began with the US Navy abolishing the time-honored tradition of serving "grog." Alcohol aboard ships of the Navy was prohibited and immediately replaced by Welch's grape juice. Sailors were not amused.

The peripatetic "Colonel" Edward House returned from a mission to Europe in June. House, who was an honorary "Texas colonel," and had never actually served in the military, was a close friend of President Wilson. The President, who was growing increasingly concerned about tensions among the European nations, had sent House on an informal, non-diplomatic "fact finding mission." House came back from visits with the Kaiser in Berlin and political leaders in France and England with the impression that Germany was "surcharged with war and warlike preparations (and) militarism run stark mad." His impression of England was that the Crown held her closest allies, France and Russia, "like a cocked gun: whenever she (England) consents, France and Russia will close in on Germany and Austria." On the surface, House's report was alarming but he incorrectly concluded that the various interests involved, although bellicose, were too occupied with commerce and internal matters to actually go to war on any grand scale. Wilson, who was not much stirred by international politics, was more than happy to accept the overly optimistic report and move on to more pressing domestic matters.

In a ceremony similar to the completion of the transcontinental railroad at Promontory Point, Utah, in 1869, the last telephone pole linking the east coast to the west coast was sunk into the ground and its wires hooked together on June 27th at the Nevada-Utah border.

Then, fateful shots rang out in Sarajevo on June 28th. The world's rapid decline into international madness began with the most unfortunate wrong-turn in automobile driving history—then or since. Archduke Franz Ferdinand, 50, heir presumptive to the throne of the Austro-Hungarian Empire, was riding in an open touring car, with his wife Sophie, on June 28, 1914, in the Serbian capital.

The Archduke was on an inspection tour in unfriendly territory roiling with political unrest. Earlier in the day, riding in the same car, the couple had narrowly escaped injury when a crude grenade rolled off the back of their limousine and exploded, injuring riders in the car behind them. After lunch, the Archduke elected to carry on with his trip to show the denizens of Serbia he could not be intimidated. His driver, however, went the wrong way. A mistaken turn took them down a side street too narrow for the big sedan. While the driver started backing up, a Serbian anarchist, sipping coffee at a sidewalk café, recognized the royal couple sitting in the rear seat. Nineteen-year old Gavrilo Princip, who happened to be carrying a loaded pistol under his coat, made a split second decision. He leapt up, ran to the car, and shot Sophie in the abdomen and then fired a bullet into the Archduke's neck. He tried to turn the gun on himself but was wrestled to the ground by a bystander before he could pull the trigger again. The Archduke and his wife were dead in minutes, both having bled to death from their wounds.

In 1914, few Americans had heard of Archduke Franz Ferdinand and even fewer understood his significance to the tangled alliances tenuously holding together the tottering crowns of Europe. When he and his wife were gunned down the world—and America—would learn in a hurry just what their murders meant to the "old order" and the new.

The killings precipitated a declaration of war by Austria-Hungary on the assassin's home state of Serbia (July 28th). With astonishing rapidity, other dominoes began to fall: pre-arranged alliances were called upon, one after another, and within weeks France, Britain, and Russia—the "Allied Nations"—were at war with Germany, Austria-Hungary and the Ottoman Empire—the "Central Powers."

The United States watched the war unravel from afar with President Wilson determined to keep America out of the conflict. The predominant sentiment among most Americans was: "It's not our fight;" but, the polyglot United States, with large ethnic communities closely tied to every warring faction, watched with eager fascination. The American business community, with interests in every belligerent nation, hoped to capitalize on the revenue possibilities without getting into any messy entanglements.

During the same summer, America was stricken with a bad case of baseball fever, which actually occupied as many headlines as the events unfolding in Europe. "The Babe," the legendary George Herman "Babe" Ruth, Jr., made his major league debut with the Boston Red Sox on July 11th. Although Ruth would make his reputation as a "slugger," he initially started as a pitcher, twice winning 23 games in a season.

On July 4th, the lowly Boston Braves were in last place in the National League. They were playing in a rented stadium (Fenway Park) while their new field was under construction. Then, something happened: the team roster, mostly journeyman players, caught fire. Their starting trio of pitchers became unstoppable. Their bats thundered. The team finished the pennant race ten-and-a-half games in front. The World Series was played against the Philadelphia Athletics October 9 to October 13: the Braves won all four games, the first four game sweep in World Series history.

There was even more baseball legend made that summer: On July 17th, at Forbes Field in Pittsburgh, the New York Giants were playing the

Pirates in a marathon game that had already gone twenty-one innings and was tied 1 to 1. The skies were rumbling with thunder and rain threatened. Outfielder Red Murray was under a fly ball that would finally win the game for the Giants, 3-to-1. At the instant he caught the ball, he was struck by lightning. Somehow, he managed to survive—and hold onto the ball—thus ending the game in electrifying fashion.

Ghosts from April's "Ludlow Massacre" returned to haunt New York City and the Rockefeller family on July 4th. On that Independence Day, at 1626 Lexington Avenue, near 103rd Street, the top three floors of a brand new tenement building were blown skyward as a large cache of dynamite exploded inside the upper floors. The dynamite was being assembled into a bomb by three anarchists who intended to use it to blow up the Rockefeller family at their Pocantico Hills home in Westchester County. The bomb went off prematurely, killing the conspirators and one other innocent woman who rented in the building. The bomb makers were later identified as members of the radical union group called Industrial Workers of the World; or, the IWW.

The IWW, widely known as the "Wobblies," earned their nickname in a humorous way: It seems that early on, during one of the IWW's first sponsored strikes in Vancouver, Canada, a local IWW supporter, who was Chinese and owned a restaurant, agreed to feed the strikers. His English was poor, apparently, and each time a hungry striker would show up, he would ask, "You Eye Wobble Wobble?" That became "Wobblies," and the nickname stuck.

On a more serious note, The Rockefellers were apparently so shaken by the events in Ludlow, and then the Lexington Street Bombing, that the family began their famous philanthropic outreach, a noble effort that has lasted to this very day. To further repair and burnish the family's reputation, they also started the very first corporate public relations initiative, spawning yet another large industry.

The events in Europe, as the war expanded, caused the closing of the New York Stock Exchange on August 1st. All of the European stock exchanges had already closed. New York followed suit fearing the collapse of stock prices entirely.

On August 6th, Dennis Patrick Dowd, Jr., enlisted in the French Foreign Legion, becoming the first American to fight in World War I. Dowd was a 1911 graduate of Columbia Law School who would later join the 170th US Infantry. In 1916, he elected to train as an aviator and was, unfortunately, killed in an aircraft accident on August 11th, 1916.

The Panama Canal was finally opened in August. Started by France in 1881, the construction of the canal, in the beginning, was an unmitigated disaster costing thousands of lives and millions of wasted francs. Most of the fatalities were due to tropical disease and the appalling working conditions. Hundreds of millions in funds disappeared due to mismanagement, political intrigue, poor engineering, and corruption. The French finally gave up—but the Americans were eager to pick up the pieces and begin anew. After some political wrangling of dubious honesty, and the creation of a whole new country (Panama) by wresting lands away from Columbia, the United States took over the construction in 1904 and finished the project ten years later. Along the way, American engineers had to devise many new methods of construction and US military sanitation officers had to conquer yellow fever. The United States spent $375 million to complete the project (equal to $8.5 billion dollars today). Fittingly, the first ship to sail through the canal was the American steamship, *SS Ancon* on August 15th.

President Wilson, in an August 19th address to the Senate, declared that the United States was committed to "The true spirit of neutrality" in regard to the widening war in Europe. Content, for the time being, to watch from afar, America moved ahead.

September 1st brought the death of the very last passenger pigeon, "Martha," at the Cincinnati Zoo. As little as fifty years prior, the passenger pigeon had existed in flocks that numbered in the billions. It was, at one time, the most common bird in the world and accounted for roughly one-quarter of all the birds in North America. The bird's demise has been attributed to the devastation of its natural habitat through de-forestation and to hunting on a massive scale: Pigeon meat was enormously popular on American tables in the 19th century. The death of Martha started a genuine debate on animal extinction that continues to this day and Martha became a rallying point for the relatively new American conservation movement.

The Federal Trade Commission was established on September 26th after years of rancorous political debate and infighting over the rights and privileges of corporations versus consumers. The FTC was a hallmark of Wilson's first term and a key goal of the so-called Progressive Era, started by President Theodore Roosevelt. The FTC was put in place to promote consumer protection and prevent anti-competitive business practices.

Four days later, on the 30th, the "Flying Squadron" came into existence. This was not some new form of military endeavor but rather the beginning of what would become the very powerful and very controversial Temperance Movement. The Flying Squadron was organized by former Indiana governor James F. Hanly and consisted of three separate groups that "barnstormed" America from September 30th to June 6th, 1915, preaching about the evils of alcohol. The Temperance Movement would be responsible for the generation of the Eighteenth Amendment to the Constitution (ratified January 16th, 1919) which effectively banned alcoholic beverages across America. The experiment was a disaster and was de-certified with the passage of the Twenty-first Amendment on December 5th, 1933.

On October 7th a joyous wedding was held that would have profound consequences on the future of the country: Joseph Patrick Kennedy, Jr., married Rose Fitzgerald, in Boston, after a seven year courtship.

In New York City, on November 4th, Vogue Magazine held its first "Model & Fashion Show."

On November 21st the brand new and architecturally innovative Yale Bowl held its very first football game. Unfortunately for the "Yalies," the visiting Harvard football team trounced the "Bulldogs" 36-0.

In late November, the new York Stock Exchange re-opened for bond trading, followed by the re-starting of stock trading on December 12th. The Dow Jones Industrial Average promptly took its largest one-day drop in history, down 24%.

Notable passings in 1914 included: Civil War general and hero of Gettysburg Joshua Lawrence Chamberlain (February 24, age 85); engineer and inventor George Westinghouse (March 12, age 67); social reformer and journalist Jacob Riis (age 65, May 26); Admiral Alfred Thayer Mahan (age 74, December 1) and naturalist John Muir (age 76, December 24).

Notable births in 1914 included: novelist Ralph Ellison; WW II hero Edward "Butch" O'Hare; Gen. William Westmoreland; Senator Edmund Muskie; actor Alec Guinness; author Bernard Malamud; boxer Joe Louis; actor E. G. Marshall; Gen. Creighton Abrams; television producer Alan Funt; fitness guru Jack LaLanne; explorer Thor Heyerdahl; poet Dylan Thomas; Dr. Jonas Salk; actor Hedy Lamarr; baseball legend Joe DiMaggio; actor Dorothy Lamour; and Sherpa Tenzing Norgay.

America's Military Posture-1914:

As war events thundered along, a small coterie of political and military leaders began to wonder if and when the vortex in Europe might suck America into its maw, and if so, how could Americas respond? At the time, the entire United States armed forces numbered far less than the armies and navies of even some of the minor players in the conflict.

As Europe, the Middle East, and (to a much lesser extent) the Far East pummeled one another during the first six months of what would become a long and devastating conflict, the United States was still standing on the sidelines. This was deemed a good thing for many reasons, not the least of which was that America was woefully unprepared for war.

From the country's earliest days, the Founding Fathers had been loath to maintain a standing army of any consequence or a navy of any real breadth and depth. Looking to their (primarily) European forebears, men like Washington, Adams, Jefferson, and Franklin had seen and even experienced the proclivity of well-armed nations with bluff and bowed navies to get themselves into one war after another, mostly at the hands of greedy monarchs or political adventurers. This is not what they wished for in regard to the new Cradle of Democracy. America's early federal administrations were content to maintain token forces at the national level and empower the individual states to maintain local militias that could be called up for national service if conditions demanded it.

Time and again, when the country had been faced with national emergencies, either from within (The Civil War) or without (1812, the Mexican War, the Spanish-American War) the nation had always been able to build up quickly to the strength necessary to battle its foes. Then, after each conflict, the natural instinct became one of demobilizing to minimal levels.

Such was the state of the US Army (but to a lesser extent the US Navy) as the Great War commenced. To protect all of its 48 states and numerous far-flung territories, the entire US Army, in July, 1914, consisted of roughly 4,500 officers and 88,500 enlisted men. This army was smaller than that of all the other combatant nations except

Portugal and Montenegro—even Belgium had 30,000 more troops.

The Army, such as it was, had obligations overseas in the Philippines, Panama, Puerto Rico and China. Only half the standing army was actually based stateside, and more than a third of that number were tied to the 117 Coastal Artillery Companies guarding the shorelines, east and west. There were a paltry 36 artillery batteries and 15 cavalry regiments. There was no organized Air Service until the Signal Corps began experimenting with airplanes in July.

The Army's standard weapons were: a collection of pistols, mostly for officers; the ubiquitous 1903, bolt-action, 5-round Springfield rifle; the Hotchkiss machine gun; the Model 1905 bayonet; and the 1913 cavalry sword fashioned by Lieutenant George Patton (a notable fencing enthusiast at West Point). Fortunately for the combat survival of the puny US Cavalry, the lance had been abandoned shortly after the start of the Civil War; but, in 1914, the standard transport and "fighting vehicle" remained the horse. The tank had not yet been invented, but the Army did have a handful of "armored cars" as well as several companies of trucks, mostly for hauling gear.

The mindset of the US Army was changing, though: Major General Leonard Wood had been Chief of Staff since April, 1910. An Indian and Spanish-American War hero who had a Medal of

Honor to his credit, he was the only medical doctor (then and since) to hold the Army's highest post. He had instituted critical reforms in the Army during his tenure but had run afoul of the "old guard" to whom change was anathema. Wood was succeeded by a caretaker Chief, Major General William Wotherspoon, another old Indian fighter, who lasted from April until November when he was mandatorily retired for age (64). The next Chief, the one who would see the Army thru the years until America declared war in 1917, was Major General Hugh Scott. General Scott was a West Pointer and another sturdy veteran of the Indian Wars. He steadily rose through the ranks and was Superintendent of West Point from 1906-1910. After his appointment as Chief, most of his energies, which were considerable, were poured into getting the US Army into a state of readiness for war. His single biggest contribution during his tenure (until September, 1917, when he, too, was of mandatory retirement age) was to get America ready for conscription. He also served as temporary Secretary of War in 1916.

The rest of the officer corps consisted of many senior majors, lieutenant colonels, and colonels of long standing: these were men who had survived the slow, arduous climb through the ranks, when promotion proceeded at a glacial pace. In the late 19th century, newly minted second lieutenants could wait ten years or more for promotion to the next step. Chief of Staff Wood had tried to institute rank advancement based on merit, but had met stubborn resistance. As a result, the top of the pile was a logjam of very senior officers who were waiting around for retirement. They held coveted slots that were blocked to younger officers of ambition and talent.

Fortunately, a number of these junior officers elected to stick around. In 1914, Douglas MacArthur was eleven years out of West Point, where he had graduated at the top of his class in 1903. After all that time, he was only a captain. George Patton, Class of 1909, was still a second lieutenant. Dwight Eisenhower and Omar Bradley were seniors at West Point.[4]

In the enlisted ranks, service in the Regular Army was not considered an "elite profession" but it was, at least, an honorable one. Due to its minimal needs, recruitment was not difficult, but it took men who had a great tolerance for long periods of boredom and a life of constant regulation. They would not get rich, either, on an average infantryman's pay of roughly $200.00 per year.

The US Navy was in better condition, but compared to the navies of the other major naval combatants, it was becoming obsolete. The recent high water mark for the Navy had been "Teddy"

---

[4] The Class of 1915, because of two world wars during their careers, would be called "the class the stars fell on." Fifty-nine of the 164 graduates in 1915 would attain general officer rank.

Roosevelt's "Great White Fleet," which had sailed around the world in the fourteen months between December, 1907, and February, 1909. Roosevelt sent sixteen battleships, 14,000 sailors, and a host of support ships to twenty ports of call. It was meant to be—and it became—a demonstration of seapower on behalf of the US Navy.

By 1914, however, the coal-fired, pre-dreadnaught battleships that had so successfully circumnavigated the globe, were being eclipsed by the new, much more powerful, oil fired dreadnaught-type battleships of the Royal and Imperial German Navies. In early 1914, the US Navy was the third largest in the world, but fading fast in light of the frantic building programs underway in Britain, Germany, France, Austria-Hungary, Italy, and Japan.

The newest battleships in England and Germany featured triple-mount, 12-inch, rapid firing guns housed in three and four turrets per ship. The engines were oil-fired, steam-driven, geared turbines which were far superior to the older coal-fired boilers. Both European powerhouse navies—England and Germany—were building battlecruisers (a faster, lighter battleship type) as well as dozens of cruisers, destroyers, and submarines.

The US Navy had no battlecruisers in the works and was falling far behind in destroyer and submarine construction. President Wilson was not convinced that a military buildup was necessary—or politically desirable—but a fistful of modern battleships were on the way; four, in fact, and the first of the new US Navy super-dreadnaughts, *USS Nevada*, BB-36, was launched on July 11th.

Before 1909, unlike the Army, the Navy did not have a single "chief" or senior naval officer; rather, leadership was vested in the admirals who headed the Navy's powerful bureaus (such as Navigation, Construction, Personnel, etc.) plus the fleet commanders afloat. Secretary of the Navy George von L. Meyer changed that in 1909 creating a "naval aide" arrangement where four senior rear admirals were each placed in charge of Operations, Materiel, Personnel, and Inspection with the head of operations a "first among equals." The 1914 Aide for Operations was Rear Admiral Bradley A. Fiske. Although little known today, Fiske was an exceptional officer. He was an innovating engineer who invented the telescopic gun sight and the aerial torpedo, just two among well over one-hundred other patents. He held many important ship commands, and was a great strategic thinker.

Secretary Meyer was replaced in 1913 by Josephus Daniels, a strong supporter and friend of President Wilson. Daniels had been a newspaper executive and was an ardent pacifist. He immediately clashed with Admiral Fiske who wrote a prescient memo in November, 1914, that said, in part, "If this country avoids war during the next five years it will be accomplished only by a happy combination of high diplomatic skill and rare good fortune." Fiske also pointed out that the Navy was nearly 20,000 men short of filling all of the open positions it had in its enlisted ranks and officer corps.

Secretary Daniels was consistent, at least, in his reluctance to prepare the Navy for war. Fiske resigned in semi-protest in April, 1915, and his job was immediately abolished by Daniels. In its place, Daniels created the modern post of Chief of Naval Operations, which, to this day, is the senior billet in the US Navy.

The United States Marines, established in 1775, were made a distinct and separate service within the Navy Department in 1834. Their origins were to serve as ship-borne infantry and emergency cannoneers; but, by the Civil War they were being placed in semi-independent regiments and detailed to guard important military installations and many of America's foreign embassies. After the Spanish-American War, their tasks also included the role of advanced (light) infantry when interventions or occupations were needed. The entire service had never been more than 18,000 men in total, and often much less—on average, 10,000.

In 1914, the Marine Corps Commandant was Major General George Barnett who held that post from February 25, 1914, until June 30, 1920. The Marines were more prepared for conflict than either the Navy or the Army having been constantly fighting in skirmishes around the globe for decades. They were such a small portion of the overall force, however, that their numbers would not make a strategic difference until expanded— which they would be, substantially, as a declaration of war grew closer.

In summary, as the summer of 1914 passed from peace into global war, the armed forces of the United States would not have been ready to assume any significant role in the conflict, had they been required to do so. Fortunately, they were not. In addition, their Commander and Chief was firmly dedicated to a posture of strict neutrality in regard to the war affairs of Europe; but, the dawn of another year would began to reverse these postures dramatically.

◉ 1914: "The True Spirit of Neutrality" in Photos and Illustrations

The Vreeland Family
Seaside, Oregon-1914

Thaddeus Vreeland, his wife Agnes, and their children pose for the camera to commemorate a family vacation. Of Dutch descent, the Vreelands were typical of the prosperous, middle-class America that existed on the cusp of the Great War.

A Ford factory production line:
an innovation that changed American
manufacturing

The finished product: a 1914 Model "T"—base
price: $550.00

Roadways were expanding but Americans drove even where they were none, such as this adventurous young man on the brink of the Grand Canyon

TO BE FILLED IN BY COLLECTOR.

List. No. ....

.... District of ....

Date received ....

Form 1040.

INCOME TAX.

THE PENALTY
FOR FAILURE TO HAVE THIS RETURN IN
THE HANDS OF THE COLLECTOR OF
INTERNAL REVENUE ON OR BEFORE
MARCH 1 IS $20 TO $1,000.
(SEE INSTRUCTIONS ON PAGE 4)

TO BE FILLED IN BY INTERNAL REVENUE BUREAU.

File No. ....

Assessment List ....

Page .... Line ....

UNITED STATES INTERNAL REVENUE.

RETURN OF ANNUAL NET INCOME OF INDIVIDUALS.

(As provided by Act of Congress, approved October 3, 1913.)

RETURN OF NET INCOME RECEIVED OR ACCRUED DURING THE YEAR ENDED DECEMBER 31, 191 ....
(FOR THE YEAR 1913, FROM MARCH 1, TO DECEMBER 31.)

Filed by (or for) .... of ....
(Full name of individual.)   (Street and No.)

in the City, Town, or Post Office of .... State of ....
(Fill in pages 2 and 3 before making entries below.)

1. GROSS INCOME (see page 2, line 12)	$	
2. GENERAL DEDUCTIONS (see page 3, line 7)	$	
3. NET INCOME	$	

Deductions and exemptions allowed in computing income subject to the normal tax of 1 per cent.

4. Dividends and net earnings received or accrued, of corporations, etc., subject to like tax. (See page 2, line 11) . . . $ ....

5. Amount of income on which the normal tax has been deducted
and withheld at the source. (See page 2, line 9, column A) . ...

6. Specific exemption of $3,000 or $4,000, as the case may be.
(See Instructions 3 and 19) . . . .

Total deductions and exemptions. (Items 4, 5, and 6) . . . . $ ....

7. TAXABLE INCOME on which the normal tax of 1 per cent is to be calculated. (See Instruction 3) . $ ....

8. When the net income shown above on line 3 exceeds $20,000, the additional tax thereon must be calculated as per schedule below:

					INCOME.		TAX.	
1	per cent on amount over $20,000 and not exceeding $50,000 . .		$		$	
2	"	"	50,000	"	"	75,000 .	....		....
3	"	"	75,000	"	"	100,000 .	....		....
4	"	"	100,000	"	"	250,000 .	....		....
5	"	"	250,000	"	"	500,000 .	....		....
6	"	"	500,000	. . . .		....		....

Total additional or super tax . . . . $ ....

Total normal tax (1 per cent of amount entered on line 7) . . $ ....

Total tax liability . . . . $ ....

The first IRS income tax form: the ubiquitous 1040, which is still in use today, although much changed

The first commercial airline flight: January 1, 1914,
St. Petersburg to Tampa

Tony Janus (R), first licensed American commercial
pilot

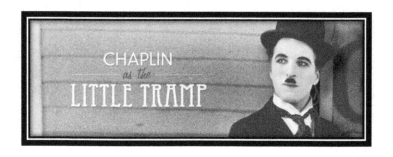

Charlie Chaplin debuts his famous character, "The Little Tramp"

US Marines and Navy Bluejackets come ashore at Veracruz in April

Bluejackets in position to storm the city

Political poster favoring US intervention in Veracruz

US Marines fighting in Veracruz

Striking coal miners and their families in the "Tent City," Ludlow, Colorado

MEMBERS OF THE COLORADO NATIONAL GUARD ENTERING THE STRIKE DISTRICT

The Colorado National Guard prepares to intervene in the Ludlow strike

Ludlow Tent City in ruins after the battle

The "Death Special" anti-striker armored car

United Mine Workers monument, Ludlow, Colorado

The cornerstone for the Lincoln Memorial is laid in February

Martha, the last passenger pigeon, dies in September

The Archduke and Grand Duchess Sophie...

...moments before the fatal shots were fired

The assassin: Serbian Gavrilo Princip, age 19

1914 World Series "fever" shares the front
page with the Great War

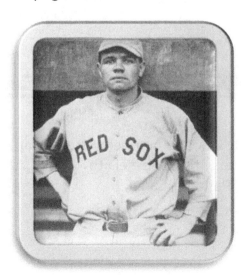

...and "Babe" Ruth begins his legendary career,
starting with the Red Sox

80-A³⁷. Opening of the Panama Canal. S.S. Ancon leaving west chamber, Gatun upper locks and entering Gatun Lake Aug 15 1914.

On August 15, the American steamship *SS Ancon* becomes the first vessel to transit the newly-completed Panama Canal.

Innovative Yale Bowl is inaugurated with its first
Harvard-Yale Game...

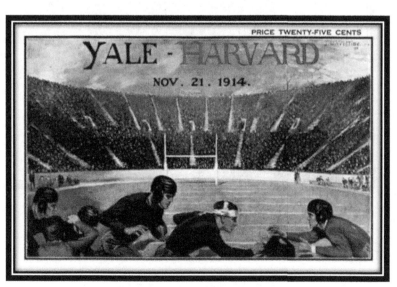

...which Harvard wins, 36-0

America begins to realize it is not prepared...

...and produces the most famous recruiting poster
in American history

⊙ 1915: The Dark Clouds of War Drift Shoreward

As 1915 opened, the war had spread fully over the face of Europe, including a Russian front, plus conflict across the Ottoman Empire and Middle East. The last of the national combatants (save the United States) joined the war as Italy sided with the Allies in May, and Bulgaria elected to fight on behalf of the Central Powers in September.

In January, Germany unleashed its latest terrifying weapon, the Zeppelin, with bombing raids over London and several coastal English cities. The huge, lumbering, airborne gas bags did little damage, at first, but as the attacks proliferated, and the Germans improved both their navigation and aiming, the destruction increased. The Kaiser was initially against bombing civilian targets, but his war council finally convinced him of the value of the psychological warfare in addition to any actual damage that might be done.

Poison gas was used for the first time, in January, against the Russians on the eastern front. The Germans then gassed the French and the Belgians, on the western front, in April. A new and sinister element was injected into modern warfare and it actually horrified all parties, even the Germans.

Germany began its first full u-boat campaign, called "unrestricted warfare," around the British isles in February. U-boat crews were freed to target any and all types of ships, civilian and military, and began to do so. In the ensuing six months, the tonnage lost exceeded that of new ships being built and caused real concern among the Allies. In retaliation, the Royal Navy imposed a total blockade against Germany, including food and humanitarian supplies.

The government of Turkey began its ruthless extermination campaign against the Armenian people in February. Over the next two years, a million and a half Armenians would be slaughtered or allowed to starve to death in the Syrian deserts.

In April, Australian and New Zealand ground forces, transported by the Royal Navy, began what turned into a disastrous invasion of Turkey via the Gallipoli Peninsula. The goal was to open a viable water route to Russia through the Black Sea. The invasion was poorly planned and mismanaged from the outset and thousands of "Aussies" and "Kiwis" lost their lives for little gain. The primary architect of this monumental failure was none other than Winston Churchill. He was, at the time, First Sea Lord, and after Gallipoli, he was forced to step down in disgrace.

On May 1st, a German u-boat sank the first American ship to be lost in the war, the tanker SS *Gulflight,* off the coast of Sicily. Six days later, in a much more troubling attack, one that will begin to change the course of American thought about the war, the *U-20* fired a single torpedo into the hull of the *RMS Lusitania*. The ship went down off the coast of Ireland in an astonishing eighteen minutes. A total of 1,198 people were lost, including 128 Americans. It was a singular moment in American history and that of the Great War.

In August, a breakthrough in airplane design and aerial firepower handed almost total domination of the skies to the Germans. It was the beginning of the so-called "Fokker scourge." The revolutionary aircraft design of the Eindecker fighter, along with a machine gun synchronized to the rotations of plane's propeller, made it the aircraft to beat. It would take the Allies another year to catch up.

Land battles continued to roil the Continent, with no side gaining any grand advantage. The war had truly settled into one of attrition, conducted mostly from trench to trench. In December, the Allies finally admitted to defeat at Gallipoli and began an orderly withdrawal.

Horrendous casualty totals were already spiraling into the millions by the end of the year.

America in 1915:

Her name struck fear in kitchens everywhere: She was "Typhoid Mary," in reality, Mary Mallon, an otherwise innocent and unassuming cook-for-hire. Born in Ireland in 1869, she came to America when she was fifteen.

Somewhere along the way, she was infected by typhoid fever, a highly infectious bacterial disease that manifests in high fevers, internal bleeding, intense discomfort; and, without effective treatment (antibiotics, mostly) could often cause death. That was not true in Mary's case, though: She proved to be a "carrier" of the disease, never becoming sick herself. Because of poor sanitation habits (all too common in her day) Mary could pass on the disease to others, and she did, primarily through her cooking. No one knows, with certainty, how many people she infected but the numbers she made sick were considerable and the people who died numbered between two and fifty, depending on whose figures were used.

Mary worked for a number of wealthy families in New York City and on Long Island from 1900 to 1915. Everywhere she went, people she cooked for came down with typhus. The health authorities became suspicious, had Mary tested, and found her gallbladder full of infection. They quarantined her for three years. Once she agreed to cease being a cook and take better precautions, she was released. At first, she became a laundress, but since that paid less than cooking, she changed her name to "Mary Brown" and was right back to her preferred profession. Her final downfall was being caught at Sloane Women's Hospital in New York City, in 1915. She was a cook there when an outbreak of typhus occurred infecting twenty-five and killing two.

She never admitted to being sick, never agreed to have her gall bladder removed (which would have "cured" her) and spent the rest of her life (another twenty-three years) in quarantine at North Brother Island in New York Harbor.

On January 12th, Rocky Mountain National Park was established by act of Congress, expanding the list of National Parks to nine. Beginning with Yellowstone Park, in 1872, the string of these preserved treasures today numbers fifty-eight with more on the way.

On the same day, the 12th, Congress failed to pass another law: This one would have given women the right to vote. Women's suffrage had been debated for decades, but had only begun to develop real traction at the beginning of the 20th Century. By 1915, four states (Idaho, Utah, Wyoming and Colorado) had enfranchised women, but pressure was developing which would ultimately result in the 19th Amendment to the Constitution in 1920. President Wilson was the first sitting president to endure a demonstration outside the White House, and it was over a woman's right to vote.

On January 28th, The United States Coast Guard, which had been organized in 1790, was merged with the US Lifesaving Service and designated a true uniformed and armed military branch. Prior to 1915, the Coast Guard had been a "revenue service," primarily responsible for collecting taxes from merchant mariners, cracking down on pirates, and rescuing distressed mariners at sea. After this change, the Coast Guard became a fighting service, which, in war, would be placed under the control of the Secretary of the Navy.

While the war ramped up in Europe, America was becoming obsessed with "the movies," and one of the most controversial and influential films of all time was released on February 8th. It was "The Birth of a Nation," directed by the movie pioneer D. W. Griffith. The themes of this first twelve-reel movie (shown with an intermission) was the Civil War, the war's aftermath, and Reconstruction in the South. The South was pictured as "victimized" by a vengeful North. Blacks in the movie were sometimes portrayed by whites in black-face makeup and the Ku Klux Klan was depicted as a heroic force for justice. Nonetheless, crowds everywhere flocked to see the film and today it remains on the American Film Institute's "One Hundred Years of Great Movies" at number 44.

Almost one year to the day after the laying of the cornerstone for the Lincoln Memorial, the first building stones were set in place on February 12th.

On February 20th, the Panama-Pacific International Exposition opened in San Francisco. This world's fair ran for the balance of the year and was held to celebrate both the completion of the Panama Canal and the re-birth of San Francisco after the devastating 1906 earthquake. Among the dozens of exhibits were pavilions dedicated to art, food, culture, transportation, agriculture, mining, and manufacturing. Over eighteen million visitors from twenty-four countries attended. Highlights included the Tower of Jewels, a 450-foot tall edifice studded with over one-hundred thousand cut-glass gems that shimmered in the sunlight during the day and twinkled like stars when illuminated by searchlights at night. There was also a miniature Panama Canal and a pavilion where one of the first transcontinental telephones was installed, allowing callers from the east coast to hear the surf crashing on the west coast.

March 3rd heralded the founding of NACA: the National Advisory Committee for Aeronautics. Only twelve years after the Wright brothers first flight, a federal agency was created to manage the design and development of aircraft technology. Hundreds of pioneering aircraft design applications came out of NACA, including the wind tunnel. NACA's role evolved constantly to keep pace with the rapid advance of aircraft design and development. Its name was changed, in 1958, to what we know it as today, NASA: the National Aeronautics and Space Administration.

On May 6th, "Babe" Ruth hit his first of 714 home runs. It was in the 3rd inning of a game at the Polo Grounds where his Red Sox were playing his future team, the Yankees. Home runs were still rarities, even more so for a pitcher, and Ruth's massive shot into the stands awed the crowd.

May 7th, after lunch in New York, the first reports of disaster began to trickle in by wireless. The world's largest, fastest, and—some said—most beautiful passenger liner, *RMS Lusitania*, was gone, sunk, eleven miles off the coast of southern Ireland. She had been only hours away from her home port of Liverpool, England. A German torpedo—or possibly torpedoes, no one knew at first—fired from a u-boat lurking nearby, had torn the ship's hull apart. Incredibly, this mighty ship, with all her steel, strength and power, sank in only eighteen minutes. Of the 1,959 passengers and crew aboard, 1,198 were lost, including 128 Americans.

Questions about the *Lusitania's* sinking still abound today, over one hundred years after she slipped beneath the waves. First among these concerns was and is: Why was she attacked at all? In February, as we noted above, Germany had declared the waters surrounding Great Britain, to be a "war zone," in which all seaborne traffic could be subject to attack; and, Germany had launched her first unrestricted u-boat campaign. Still, ships that were obviously of no military value or unlikely to carry military cargoes were generally given a pass. Even for a novice u-boat commander (which the captain of the *U-20* was not—he was highly capable and experienced), the recognition profile for such a large and well-known ship could hardly have been more obvious; yet, she was attacked anyway.

Part of the answer may lie in the fact, known to the German Navy, that the *Lusitania* was a designated Royal Navy reserve combatant. Though not armed with any guns, she could, in time of war, carry significant amounts of materiel or troops. On her ill-fated 202nd Atlantic crossing the German high command believed—correctly, as it turned out—that *Lusitania* had tons of ammunition and war supplies in her hold, all destined for the British Army. That made her, in the world of the Kreigsmarine, a legitimate target. There was also a rumor—untrue—that she was ferrying troops from Canada destined for the trenches in France.

Another and more curious part of the war equation was that *Lusitania* was completely unguarded. On other voyages, and even with other liners, the Royal Navy had sent along escort ships, principally destroyers, to shepherd valuable vessels to safe harbors. This was not the case for *Lusitania* this time, which had to have made her a more tempting target for any ambitious u-boat skipper.

Why would anyone reserve passage on a ship like *Lusitania* during these troubled times? The German Consulate in New York, from whence *Lusitania* sailed on her last voyage, had gone so far as to post advertisements in the New York newspapers warning potential passengers as to the u-boat danger; yet, people still booked.

It seems almost no one believed a civilized people, like the Germans, would be so crass as to attack a peaceful, unarmed passenger liner. Those sorts of things were just not done. Then, of course, it was common knowledge that the powerful *Lusitania*, with her top speed of 25 knots, could outrun any u-boat, and that was true. People also had confidence in the liner's size, strength, and the bulk of her steel hull. Even though the *Titanic* disaster was still fresh in the minds of the sailing crowd, many improvements—including more lifeboats—had been made since 1912. All in all, those taking passage on the *Lusitania* had little reason to be overly concerned—or so they thought.

Why did such a large vessel sink so rapidly, and after being hit by only one torpedo? The munition the *U-20* fired into the starboard hull of the Lusitania, just below the wheelhouse, forward, was packed with about 90 pounds of TNT. That would certainly be enough to punch a sizeable hole into the hull, and an explosion was definitely experienced, but reasonable efforts at damage control or counter flooding among the ship's compartments ought to have allowed *Lusitania* to keep on sailing, at least for an hour or more—perhaps even long enough to reach Liverpool. The initial blast, however, was quickly followed by a second explosion, within the hull, one of much larger magnitude. This blast ripped the starboard hull apart and created a gaping hole so large that even the mighty *Lusitania* could not recover from its impact. The ship listed to starboard 30° immediately and started to sink.

There has been speculation for many years that the munitions that *Lusitania* carried caused the secondary explosion that doomed the ship. Later analysis revealed, however, that the contraband cargo was not located in that area of the hold. The current operating theory, and a more plausible one, is that coal dust was the culprit. *Lusitania* was at the end of her voyage and much of her coal, used to fire her boilers, was depleted. Coal dust would have been rampant and researchers now believe that the torpedo's blast ignited the combustible dust thereby generating a second massive explosion.

Given all the shipboard improvements, and the addition of more lifeboats and life rafts since the *Titanic* disaster, why was the loss of life so great? Time was the mortal enemy, and the additional lifeboats and rafts did not matter: There was too little time between the attack and the sinking to organize an effective evacuation of the passengers and crew. The ship was crippled so badly, listing over so quickly, that it was impossible to launch many of the lifeboats. Half were already under water on the starboard side, and the other half were so precariously perched on the elevated port side that when they were released they plunged into the sea and smashed up immediately. Although the water was relatively shallow (*Lusitania's* bow hit the bottom before her stern sunk beneath the surface) it was fatally cold: many of the victims died of hypothermia.

The loss of *Lusitania* outraged many Americans. It was the very first major lightning strike for the United States in considering whether to become involved in the war. The White House was flooded with letters and telegrams decrying the atrocity and the President was personally furious. Wilson was not moved to strike back, however: at least not then. In actuality, most of America concurred with their President. Although much has been written about the outrage expressed, the majority of Americans, even after the sinking of the *Lusitania*, were still not in favor joining the war.

War fever was, however, escalating in certain quarters. Former President Theodore Roosevelt was leading a charge favoring "getting in." Also on Roosevelt's side was former Army Chief of Staff General Leonard Wood and the Republican Senate minority leader, Massachusetts senator Henry Cabot Lodge. President Wilson still proclaimed that he was "too proud to fight," words that enraged Roosevelt and fanned the flames of war preparedness even higher. Many American businesses weren't too proud to get involved, though, and a number of manufacturing companies began switching over to the production of war materiel in order to take advantage of easy profits.

Wilson came under growing pressure but he knew, unlike most, that American arms were still unprepared to assume the duties that would be required if the nation went to war. He also knew that he could not appear to be weak, either at home or abroad. Wilson sent what he believed was a proper and "measured" response to Germany: He demanded that Germany rescind its declared war against unarmed merchant ships, and if they would not, then he would pursue war aims. Wilson's message saddened his Secretary of State, the pacifist William Jennings Bryan, who promptly resigned in protest on June 9th.

Even though the tragedy of the *Lusitania* failed to breach the dike of isolationism holding American back, cracks appeared in the wall of resolve to stay out of it—deep cracks. A silent sense of inevitability started to seep through the breaks and one of the most visible signs that feelings were changing came from a group of private citizens, most of whom had been in the government at some point. Encouraged by war advocates like Roosevelt, Wood, and former secretaries of war Elihu Root and Henry Stimson, a number of "citizens military training camps" sprang up around the country. These encampments, held in the summer months, started a movement that attracted thousands of men, mostly from the upper classes of American society, and especially "gentlemen" from the country's elite schools. In what turned into a program for "older boy scouts," the cream of society lived in tents, ate in mess halls, and marched day and night learning the rudiments of what the military would normally require as "basic officer training." The most prominent of these summer camps, which lasted about four weeks, was in Plattsburgh, New York— close enough to, yet far enough away from, the canyons of money and power in New York City, Boston and Washington, DC.

Quietly yet effectively, and paid for by each attendee, a cadre of thousands of men who could become junior officers was being prepared for a war that just about all of them believed to be inevitable. Camps like Plattsburgh, Gettysburg, Pennsylvania, and Pacific Grove near Monterrey, California, formed the heart of what would become known as the "Preparedness Movement." Former President Roosevelt would write about the camps thusly: "The military tent, where boys sleep side by side, will rank next to the public school among the great agents of democracy." Three of Roosevelt's four sons, Ted, Jr., Quentin, and Kermit, would all rotate through Plattsburgh.

Ten weeks after the *Lusitania* suffered its grim fate, another passenger vessel sank with a terrible loss, this time claiming 844 lives. Unlike the *Lusitania,* though, this ship was not at sea, but on a lake; it was not steaming ahead but standing still; and, most bizarrely of all, it was not in any imminent danger, such as from a u-boat. It was, in fact, tied up to a dock when it suddenly rolled on its side and went under. This is the strange case of the steamer *SS Eastland*, a tour boat that normally plied the Great Lakes, hauling up to 2,500 passengers at a time on holiday excursions.

The *Eastland* had been constructed in 1902 and from the very outset, she had problems with her center of gravity and top-heaviness. On a number of occasions, the crew of the ship had to take emergency measures to correct alarming lists when too many passengers congregated on one side of the ship or the other. Nonetheless, the *Eastland* continued to operate and conducted hundreds of successful cruises on the Great Lakes from her home port in Chicago.

On the morning of July 24th, though, something went terribly wrong. The ship had been chartered, along with two others, to take thousands of Western Electric workers on a day-long excursion and company picnic. The ship had loaded its maximum complement of passengers (2,572) by 6:30 AM. Scores of people went to the top deck to enjoy the view, with many more electing to stay inside on a cool and damp morning. For some reason, at 7:10 AM, a large group of passengers moved from the starboard side to the port side of the top deck. The *Eastland* immediately began rolling slowly to the left and nothing the crew tried could right the ship. The *Eastland* settled on its port side and sank, trapping hundreds of people below decks, some crushed to death by shifting furniture and heavy equipment.

The *Eastland* tragedy was the largest loss of life from a single shipwreck in the history of shipping on the Great Lakes. Six people, including the owner of the steamship company and the ship's captain, were indicted for manslaughter or criminal carelessness. At a subsequent trial, all were found not guilty, principally because the ship had sustained such a long career without incident prior to this accident.

The *Eastland* was raised from the bottom of the Chicago River and given a new life: as a US Navy reserve training ship, which she remained until after WW II. In August, 1943, she served as host to President Franklin Roosevelt and his senior aides on a ten-day Great Lakes strategic planning cruse. One can only wonder what the President was thinking as the resurrected *Eastland* sailed away from the dock.

On July 28th, three-hundred and thirty US Marines stormed ashore at Port-au-Prince, Haiti, to begin a military occupation of that island nation that would wax and wane over the next two decades, finally ending in 1934. The primary impetus for this incursion was political instability in the country, which had seen six changes in the presidency in just four years. Instability was not good for the significant American business interests and investments in Haiti; plus, President Wilson was very concerned about the growing influence of Germany in the Haitian banking, business, and political communities. To Wilson, the German interference was a very vexing violation of the long-standing Monroe Doctrine. The Marines met minimal resistance (only one Haitian soldier lost his life) and there were no Marine casualties.

Over a two week period, from August 5th until the 23rd, separate hurricanes ravaged Galveston, Texas and New Orleans, leaving 275 dead and extensive property damage in both municipalities.

One of the lowest points in the sad history of anti-Semitism in America occurred on August 17th. A thirty-one year old Jewish engineer and head of the National Pencil Factory in Atlanta, Georgia, Leo Frank, had been convicted two years prior of the brutal rape and murder of one of his young employees, thirteen year old Mary Phagan. There was only circumstantial evidence that Frank had committed the crime, and strong evidence leading to at least two other local men. Frank, from Brooklyn, and a graduate of Cornell, was viewed in the South as a "carpet-bagging Northern capitalist" by many in his adopted state; plus, he was a Jew. There was a strong undercurrent of anti-Semitism throughout the trial and subsequent appeal proceedings. When the governor of Georgia commuted Frank's death sentence to one of life imprisonment, based on the scant physical evidence, there was an outcry among the local citizenry.

Frank survived a prison throat-slashing attack in May, and was still in the prison hospital when twenty-five armed men stormed the jail and dragged Frank away on August 17th. He was driven over one hundred miles to near where Mary Phagan's family lived, and lynched from a nearby tree. Photographs of the horrifying hanging were turned into local postcards, and the noose used to string Frank up was cut into souvenir pieces.

Many decades later, evidence finally surfaced, in the form of a dying declaration, that Frank was not the killer. A witness had seen another man, the factory janitor, carrying Mary Phagan's body to the basement where she was later found. The State of Georgia still refused to reverse Frank's conviction, but finally agreed, in 1986, to issue him a posthumous pardon.

The tensions and conflicts in Mexico that had been boiling since 1910, in the form of continual revolution, reached a milestone on October 19th when the US Government finally recognized the government of Venustiano Carranza. Carranza had overthrown Victoriano Huerta, whose administration the US had opposed with its invasion of Veracruz in 1914. In the middle of this mix, however, lurked two other revolutionaries who would have a significant impact on Mexican events in the years immediately ahead: Pancho Villa and Emiliano Zapata.

The infamous Ku Klux Klan, a pro-Southern organization founded by ex-Confederates after the Civil War, sprang up in Tennessee late in 1865. The goals the loosely amalgamated chapters of the Klan espoused were mostly centered on white supremacy and keeping African-Americans from achieving voting rights. To those ends, the Klan had a bloody and violent decade or so before a Federal government crackdown led to its effective disintegration by the mid-1870's. This was not the final end of the Klan, however.

The Second Ku Klux Klan was organized in late 1915 and officially founded at Stone Mountain, Georgia, on November 27th, Thanksgiving evening. The "new" Klan's founder, William Joseph Simmons, a church educator from Alabama, claimed to have been inspired to rejuvenate the Klan by the movie "The Birth of a Nation," as profiled in the previous chapter. The Klan even adopted the regalia, garb, and symbols shown in the movie, which included burning crosses. This time around, the Klan was not simply anti-Black, but decidedly anti-immigrant, anti-Catholic, anti-Semitic, and in favor of Prohibition.

As the year drew to a close, pressure was beginning to mount on President Wilson to take steps to expand the military. Sentiment was not yet in favor of jumping into the war, but people were concerned what might happen if we were dragged into it. The year had seen many instances where United States interests had been attacked, especially at sea. "Preparedness" became a key watchword and a reason that the minority clamoring for war got a hearing on their concerns.

On December 7th, President Wilson delivered his Third Annual Message to Congress ("Annual Messages" were the predecessors to what we call today the President's "State of the Union" address). In it, he asked the Congress for funds to expand the army, the navy, and the merchant marine. The President couched his requests in terms of maintaining the peace, but there was little doubt he was beginning to tilt the American military towards war.

Nota Bene:

Notable passings in 1915 included, from the Lusitania disaster; writer Justus Forman, theater producer Charles Frohman, writer Elbert Hubbard, playwright Charles Klein, sportsman-philanthropist Alfred Gwynne Vanderbilt; and, from elsewhere, educator Booker T. Washington.

Those of note born in 1915 included: actress Ann Sheridan, WW II bomber pilot Paul Tibbets (the *Enola Gay*), actor Zero Mostel, bluesman Muddy Waters, jazz singer Billie Holiday, actor and director Orson Welles, Nobel economist Paul Samuelson, novelist Saul Bellow, banker David Rockefeller, Peace Corps founder Sargent Shriver and crooner Frank Sinatra.

◉ 1915: The Dark Clouds of War Drift Shoreward-Photos and Illustrations

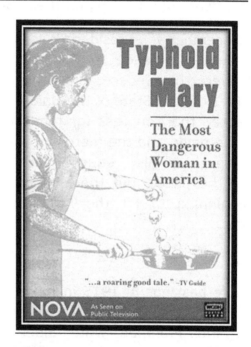

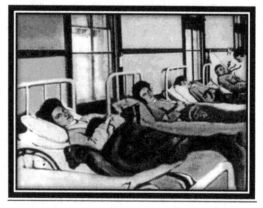

Mary Mallon, "Typhoid Mary." (foreground)
In quarantine, North Brother Island, NY

1915 poster for Women's Suffrage
Congress fails to pass legislation in favor in
February

"The Birth of a Nation"
Debuts in February to record crowds of movie
goers

The Pan-Pacific International Exposition opens
February 20th in San Francisco

RMS Lusitania-New York Harbor, early 1915

The *U-20*, sailing from port toward the Irish Sea, April, 1915

Kapitanlieutnant Walter Schweiger, Commanding Officer, *U-20*

RMS Lusitania begins to sink after being torpedoed

A fanciful contemporary depiction of the sinking

A powerful contemporary recruiting poster depicting an innocent mother and child from the *Lusitania* drowning together as the ship went down.

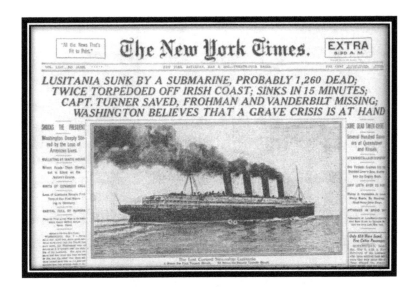

The sinking as reported by the *New York Times*

A mass burial in Ireland for some of the victims

Contemporary posters advertising the training available for young men at "summer camp" in Plattsburgh, New York-1915

"Company E"-Plattsburgh-1915

SS Eastland-1911

SS Eastland immediately after the 1915
disaster at the dock

The US Marines occupy Haiti in July

A hurricane destroys Galveston, TX, in August

Mary Phagan
The Victim

Leo Frank
The Accused

The lurid headlines after a lynch mob takes Leo
Frank from custody

The mob that kidnapped and lynched Leo Frank

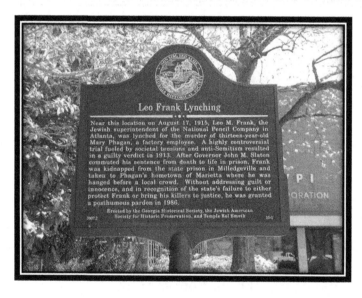

The monument erected to commemorate Leo Frank's pardon

The Four Principal Personalities of the 1915 Mexican Revolution

Venustiano Carranza   Victoriano Huerta

Emiliano Zapata   Pancho Villa

William J. Simmons-Founder of the "Second Ku Klux Klan"

Klan rally, Atlanta, GA-1915

⦿ 1916: "He Has Kept Us Out of War"

War Update:

Many of the first troops to join the fight went off to war in mid-1914 with an attitude of, "We'll beat them and be home by Christmas." By the beginning of 1916, that optimism was long gone and all sides had settled in for a protracted struggle. 1916 would be a very bad year all around: Casualties would be staggeringly high among all combatants. The largest naval battle of the war—Jutland—would be fought in the North Sea on the last day of May and first day of June. Two of the war's biggest and longest land battles would erupt during the year: the Battle of Verdun would start on February 21st and not conclude until December 18th and when the butcher's bill was totaled, it would enumerate over one million casualties. The Battle of the Somme would start July 1st and not end until November 18th. It, too, would tally over a million casualties including the largest loss of British soldiers in history—over 600,000.

Romania and Italy entered the war on the side of the Allies but Germany immediately crushed the Romanian army then fell on the Italians, pummeling them everywhere. The Russian army, on the other hand, did surprisingly well, almost knocking Austria-Hungary out of the war. In the Middle East, the Ottoman Empire suffered several major defeats including several engineered by the legendary British officer T. E. Lawrence. Bulgaria came in on the side of the Central Powers.

The United States was still on the sidelines. President Wilson, in a crucial election year, campaigned on a platform of neutrality. It was nearly his undoing. America still got her nose bloodied, though: The Army was sent into Mexico to chase down Pancho Villa. He proved to be an elusive foe and escaped one trap after another, which caused immense frustration. The Marines went storming back into Haiti and also invaded Santo Domingo. American shipping was still being attacked by German u-boats and the President was forced to take a tough "stop-or-else" line with the Kaiser.

America's Year:

As one might imagine, the 1913 imposition of the income tax, via the 16th Amendment, and the establishment of the IRS was not the most popular legislation ever enacted by the US Congress. It seemed to be only a matter of time before a legal challenge was mounted, and it finally came courtesy of Mr. Frank Brushaber, a stockholder of the Union Pacific Railroad. Mr. Brushaber sued to bar the Union Pacific from paying taxes to the government, as required under the new laws. On January 24th, the United States Supreme Court handed down an 8-0 decision (one Justice abstaining) upholding the government's right to impose and collect an income tax.

Paris felt the sting of what London had been experiencing for some months. On January 29th German zeppelins bombed the City of Light for the first time. As in London, the damage was more psychological than physical.

On February 11th, Emma Goldman was placed under arrest in New York City for violating the Comstock Law. Goldman was a leading anarchist in her day (1869-1940) and had already earned widespread notoriety in America for a number of activist causes. The Comstock Act (1873) was an "Act of the Suppression of Trade in, and Circulation of, Obscene Literature and Articles of Immoral Use." Goldman, at the time of her arrest, was lecturing on the use of contraceptives.

The Battle of Verdun began on February 21st. Americans watched from afar, as hundreds of thousands of soldiers from France and Germany went at each other in a maelstrom of massed artillery, bombs, and poison gas. The action raged across the banks of the Meuse River, near the city of Verdun, in northeastern France. The Germans attempted to capture the heights in and around the city hoping to use those positions to hurl massive amounts of artillery down on the French defenders. The results were mixed, thanks to the stout defense put up by the French and the intervention of some extremely bad weather. The contest went back and forth across the river for months before the Germans were forced to withdraw troops and send them to the Battle of the Somme. One village,

Fleury, changed hands sixteen times during an eight week period. When the contest finally concluded (in a French victory) it had lasted 303 days, totaled almost one million casualties, and had become the costliest single battle in human history.

A dark chapter in Mexican-American relations started to open in March: On the 8th and 9th, the revolutionary forces of Pancho Villa crossed the border into Columbus, New Mexico. Villa had recently suffered a serious setback, militarily, and was in desperate need of supplies and ammunition. He was also incensed at President Wilson for abandoning his cause. Wilson had, at first supported Villa against the government of President Carranza, then changed his mind. Villa's spies had told him that Columbus was defended by only one detachment of soldiers, about thirty troopers from the 13th Cavalry.

Villa and his men attacked in the pre-dawn hours of March 9th. Although taken by surprise, the Americans quickly rallied. The cavalrymen of the 13th actually numbered over three hundred, not thirty, and they were joined by dozens of civilians who took up the fight to defend their homes. Although Villa claimed victory (and hauled off a large stash of food, weapons, and mules) he lost nearly twenty percent of his force. The defenders suffered a comparatively light tally of only eight cavalrymen and citizens killed and six wounded.

More critical for Villa than his sizeable losses, however, was the ire he provoked in Washington. On March 15th, President Wilson detailed 12,000 troops to Mexico (with President Carranza's reluctant approval) under orders to capture the elusive outlaw. The very next day, March 16th, the 7th and 10th Cavalry Regiments saddled up and started moving across the border. The entire expedition was placed under the command of Brigadier General John J. "Black Jack" Pershing.

Pershing—who earned his nickname when he commanded the Black troops of the 10th Cavalry, the famous Buffalo Soldiers—spent nearly a year chasing Villa. He never captured him, or even maneuvered him into a pitched battle, but he stopped Villa from attacking American interests along the border and also kept the old rogue on the defensive. Pershing was severely hampered during his Mexican operations by an inept and seriously deficient quartermaster operation. He was constantly under-supplied, but nevertheless managed to keep nearly 10,000 men in the field, fed them, and somehow got sufficient arms and ammunition. Pershing was also operating under a dark personal cloud: Barely one year prior, he had lost his beloved wife, Helen, and three of his four children in a tragic fire at the Pershing's quarters at the Presidio in San Francisco. He never really recovered emotionally from this devastating loss.

The military challenges that Pershing faced in Mexico ultimately served a higher purpose: It taught the Army valuable lessons about field maneuvers that it would put to use in Europe in two years time. It honed the skills of a number of officers who would lead that American Expeditionary Force, including Pershing himself, along with an irrepressible young cavalry officer by the name of George Patton.

President Wilson addressed the US Congress on the u-boat war on April 19th: Germany, having declared unrestricted u-boat warfare in February, received an ultimatum from the President. Wilson declared publicly, for the first time, that if the u-boats continued un-checked, he would have no choice but to sever diplomatic relations.

On April 20th, the Chicago Cubs played their very first game at what would become known as Wrigley Field. They beat the Cincinnati Reds in eleven innings, 7-6.

The Imperial German government responded to President Wilson's u-boat ultimatum on May 4th by withdrawing its "unrestricted" u-boat policy. Henceforth, the German government declared, a "clear warning" would be given before any ship was torpedoed. Germany's Naval Minister, Admiral von Tirpitz, was outraged; and, later, blamed the loss of the war to the abandonment of this policy.

Racism reared its ugly head again in a disgraceful lynching incident on May 15th in Waco, Texas. A black farm worker in his teens, Jesse Washington, was accused of raping and murdering the wife of his employer. He confessed his crime but there is some evidence that coercion was involved. He was put on trial for all of an hour and the jury took but four minutes to convict him. As he was being led to jail, he was grabbed up by a local crowd who dragged him outside, stripped him, put a chain around his neck, and hung him on a tree outside the Waco Courthouse. It is not known to this day if he was truly guilty, but the photographs of the ugly, grisly, hanging and subsequent burning of his body, shocked America. None of the mob perpetrators were ever prosecuted.

The US Marines were ordered into the Dominican Republic on May 16th. The political situation in the Dominican had been unstable for some time. Since obtaining independence (1848) the country had seen fifty different presidents and nineteen different constitutions. The national debt, owed mostly to the United States, was out of control; and, because of that, and the nation's proximity to the newly opened and valuable Panama Canal, the Marines were sent. America would be there for the next eight years.

The *Saturday Evening Post* published the first of its many Norman Rockwell covers (*Boy with Baby Carriage*) on May 20th.

A decision in the whimsical sounding case of <u>*United States vs. Forty Barrels and Twenty Kegs of Coca Cola*</u> was handed down by the US Supreme

Court on May 22nd. The Coca-Cola Company had once touted, when still using cocaine as part of its formula for Coke, that it "cured headaches," among other remedies. The newly created Food and Drug Administration went after Coca-Cola for false advertising and product liability claims. The company had stopped using coca leaves, but the soda still contained caffeine, which the FDA believed was harmful; so, it seized a shipment (the "forty barrels and twenty kegs" referred to) and sued. After much back-and-forth in the lower courts, the company prevailed before the Supreme Court and Coke still contains caffeine.

Over two days, May 31st and June 1st, the largest naval battle of the war took place in the North Sea near the Jutland Peninsula, off the western coast of Denmark. For many months, the numerically superior Royal Navy had maintained an effective blockade of German ports in and around the North Sea. The German Navy's High Seas Fleet, commanded by Vice Admiral Reinhard Scheer, was ordered by the Kaiser to try and break the encirclement.

Against daunting odds, Scheer crafted a plan to lure the Royal Navy's battlecruiser fleet into a trap. Scheer maneuvered to steam a group of his battlecruisers across the Royal Navy's flanks believing (correctly) this would tempt the British to engage. Scheer also secretly placed a line of hidden German u-boats between himself and the British. The hope was to squeeze the Royal Navy in a pincer of surface ships and submarines. The British managed to intercept some of the German radio signals, however, and when the plan was discovered, the Royal Navy's Grand Fleet, under Admiral Sir John Jellicoe, came racing in behind the British battlecruisers commanded by Vice Admiral Sir David Beatty. The German plan still might have worked but the British passed over the German submarines before they had received their final battle orders. The result was to leave 250 surface ships—battleships, battlecruisers, cruisers, light cruisers, destroyers and torpedo boats—all in the same general vicinity and armed to the teeth. An epic surface engagement and running gun battle ensued.

When the smoke cleared two days later, the Royal Navy had lost three battlecruisers (two of which blew up with horrific losses), three cruisers, eight destroyers, and over six thousand sailors killed. The German Navy had suffered losing one battlecruiser, one battleship, four light cruisers, five torpedo boats (destroyers), and over twenty-five hundred dead. Both sides claimed victory though many experts rated the overall outcome as "indecisive." The German strategy was to destroy more British tonnage than they lost; which, from the raw numbers was a goal they achieved. However, the rate at which the losses mounted for the Germans demonstrated that the ultimate goal of outlasting the Royal Navy was not attainable. Plus, from the British side, when the battle was over, the German High Seas Fleet had been forced to slink back into port, which is where the British wanted them to be—and where they stayed, for the most part, for the balance of the war.

On the same day, June 1st, Louis Brandeis was sworn in as an Associate Justice of the US Supreme Court. A remarkable term of twenty-three years began, which included some of the most important and controversial cases in the Court's history.

Reacting to pressure for American intervention in the Great War by the Preparedness Movement, Congress passed, on June 3rd, the National Defense Act of 1916. The Regular Army would be expanded to 175,000 with a new allocation of 450,000 for the National Guard. The law gave the President the authority to call up the National Guard in times of national emergency and it also established the Reserve Officer Training Corps. The new legislation brought into being the Army's first Air Division, and included $17 million dollars for 375 new aircraft. Separately, the bill also authorized funds to build two nitrate plants: Nitrate was critical to the production of munitions. Although this was a substantial upgrade to American arms, it was far less than would be required for the United States to field an army for participation in the war abroad; thus, the isolationists considered it a partial victory as well.

On June 5th, England suffered another terrible war loss when the armored cruiser *HMS*

Hampshire struck a German mine off the Scottish Orkney Islands and sank quickly, with the loss of nearly all hands. On board was Lord Kitchener, the famous old warrior and Field Marshall. He was, at the time, British Secretary of State for War. He had been detached on a mission to Russia and was on his way there when tragedy struck. He was lost with his entire staff along with 600 crewmen from the *Hampshire*.

On June 15th, President Wilson signed the bill incorporating the Boy Scouts of America. Although the BSA had been founded in 1910, on Lord Baden-Powell's model, it was not officially chartered as a Title 36 Congressional patriotic organization until this date.

July 1st saw the beginning of the monumental Battle of the Somme, in France. From this date until November 18th, when the battle officially concluded, over one million men would become casualties. The British lost nearly 60,000 on the first day, almost 20,000 of them killed, the bloodiest day in the Commonwealth's history. Although ultimately tallied as an Allied victory, the Somme Offensive became a new benchmark for "mud, blood and futility." After nearly 625,000 casualties, The Allies gained a total of six miles of territory over a sixteen mile front: the German Army tallied 465,000 casualties defending their lines.

Was this the inspiration for "Jaws?" Between July 1st and July 12th, a series of bizarre shark attacks occurred along the New Jersey coastline resulting in four deaths and the mauling of a fifth young man who lost his left leg. Both bull sharks and great white sharks were blamed, but it was fairly clear that the terror was not the work of one lone "man-eater." The incidents passed into both legend and history and were said to have been the genesis for Peter Benchley's much later work that spawned a series of books and movies.

On July 15th, William Boeing founded a company that he called, at first, Pacific Aero Products. It later changed its name to honor its pioneering chief and became Boeing, Inc.

A measure of how powerful opinions were for and against the war made itself manifest on July 22nd. San Francisco hosted, on that day, the largest parade in its history: there were over 51,000 marchers, fifty-two bands, and 2,134 organizations in the three and a half hour affair. The parade was in celebration of 1916's Preparedness Day. About a half hour into the parade, however, a time bomb went off just south of Market Street near the landmark Ferry Building. The steel pipe full of TNT and metal slugs killed ten and wounded forty. The parade had been organized by the Chamber of Commerce and the very anti-union San Francisco business community. The perpetrators were believed to have been unionists, or perhaps anarchists. Two union leaders were tried and convicted, but their sentences were later overturned due to prosecutorial misconduct and lack of hard evidence. The actual bomber or bombers were never discovered.

A scant eight days later, on the opposite coast, German saboteurs successfully detonated an explosion at the Black Tom munitions depot in Jersey City, New Jersey. Black Tom, originally a small island next to Liberty Island, and named after either a former slave who lived there or because of its tom-cat shape, had become a major shipping point for munitions headed for the war in Europe. The presence of dynamite, artillery shells, and bullets, amounting to two million pounds, all headed to the Allied cause, did not sit well with Germany. The Kaiser's spy network in America, which was extensive, set about to destroy the cache. At two in the morning on July 30, several saboteurs successfully lit fires aboard a barge containing 100,000 pounds of TNT. Eight minutes later, the barge exploded in a massive blast which set off secondary explosions all over the depot. The nearby Statue of Liberty sustained $100,000 in damage. Thousands of windows were blown out in lower Manhattan. The stained glass windows at St. Patrick's Cathedral were destroyed and the Brooklyn Bridge swayed in the night. People twenty-five miles away thought they were experiencing an earthquake; and, in fact, the explosion was equal to a 5.0 on the Richter Scale. The actual tally of the dead is still unknown since anyone near the blast was vaporized; but, at least seven people who were known to be in the area, including the captain of the barge, were never seen again.

Although the actual loss of life was thankfully small, this act of terror inflamed anti-German passions across America. Much like the 2001 attack on New York's Twin Towers, it was seen, at the time, as an affront to American sovereignty and a terrible crime against innocent civilians. The event further pushed sentiment toward joining the war.

The Preparedness Movement continued to grow. The Plattsburg-type summer camps for "young gentlemen" continued to flourish. So many businessmen from prominent companies and the canyons of power in Manhattan flocked to the Plattsburgh enclave that it became known, in jest, as the "Tired Businessmen's Camp," in reference both to who attended, and how they felt after a long day of digging trenches and hefting 60-pound packs on long hikes. The number of men trained at all the camps around the country, presumably to become junior officers, was approaching 40,000— almost half as many men as had been in the entire US Army just three years prior.

As the warm summer days passed, the war continued to exact its tolls. The British Army in the Middle East made significant conquests over the crumbling Ottoman Empire during the first week in August. Portugal joined the conflict on the Allied side on August 7th, as did the Kingdom of Romania on August 27th. Germany promptly retaliated by declaring war on Romania the next day. Italy came in on the side of the Allies on the 28th, cheering the significant Italian-American population, and brining additional pressure on Wilson's government to support the Allied cause.

On August 9th, Lassen Volcanic National Park was established, in California, and on August 25th, President Wilson signed a bill creating the National Park Service. Although a National Park system was becoming well established, it had been under-funded for many years and infrastructure in most of the early parks had deteriorated badly. A Park Service with policing powers, a coordinated budget, and construction authority was needed to manage the millions of acres and extraordinarily beautiful sights that the parks protected. America—and her natural heritage—would finally have such an organization.

In late September, the tank was deployed in combat for the first time—with decidedly mixed results. The Battle of the Somme dragged on, adding divisions from Canada and New Zealand to the carnage.

Margaret Sanger opened the first birth control clinic in America on October 16th. The Brooklyn clinic offered services to any woman seeking birth control information for a fee of ten cents.

After a long and particularly partisan political season, the 1916 national elections were held on November 7th. Woodrow Wilson had campaigned on the slogan "He kept us out of war." Although Wilson likely believed that it was probable the United States would get in it, he also knew that the majority of Americans were still in favor of staying out of it. His Republican opponent, Supreme Court Chief Justice Charles Evans Hughes, did not advocate for direct intervention either, but he campaigned hard on "making the necessary preparations for war, should it come." The election was clearly a referendum on involvement, and Wilson eked out a very narrow victory. Although he won by 600,000 votes out of seventeen and a half million cast, the electoral college vote was a relative squeaker: 277 to 254.

During the same election, Republican Jeanette Rankin of Montana became the first woman elected to the US House of Representatives. Women still did not have a national right to vote, which made her election all the more remarkable (although women did have voting rights in Montana and about 39 other states). During her one term (she opted to run for the US Senate in 1918 and lost in the primaries) she became the only woman to vote for the 19th Amendment, which finally granted women the right to vote.

On November 18th, the commander of British forces in France, General Sir Douglas Haig, "called off" the Battle of the Somme, effectively ending the costly carnage without a concrete result.

On November 21st, the steamship *Britannic* hit a German mine near Kea, Greece, and sank. *Britannic* was the sister ship of *RMS Titanic* (and *RMS Olympic*) but had not been finished by the time war broke out. She was laid up for several months until the British government decided to take possession of her and turn her, temporarily, into a hospital ship. She was clearly marked as such, in her all-white paint and red crosses, but underwater mines could not discriminate on any basis. Fortunately, nearly all of her crew, medical personnel, and patients were rescued during the hour it took her to sink. She was the largest single ship (48,158 gross tons) to be lost in the war.

In December, in the Dolomite Region of northern Italy, the Austrians and Italians were engaged in intense combat in harsh winter conditions. On the 13th, atmospheric conditions and previous heavy snowfalls combined to create a disaster unique unto even that bizarre war. A series of avalanches—some reports say there were as many as one hundred—wiped away somewhere in the vicinity of 10,000 Austrian and Italian troops clinging to the mountainsides. Entire barracks filled with sleeping soldiers were tossed down from steep heights into the valleys below. Whole regiments were swept away as millions of tons of snow, ice, and rock hurtled down from above. It was an unmitigated disaster. Some men survived even though trapped for several days under mounds of snow. Some men weren't found for decades, when receding glaciers eventually gave up frozen corpses still perfectly preserved down to their polished buttons and the brightly colored ribbons on their tunics.

On December 18th, the Battle of Verdun is declared over—a victory for the French. Four days later the plucky Sopwith Camel makes its maiden flight in combat. This new generation Allied fighter is the intended antidote for the fearsome German Fokker aircraft.

President Wilson issued a "peace note" to all the warring nations on December 18th, requesting that they state their ultimate aims for having gone to war. It was a gambit from the President to put himself in the position of chief mediator once the war began to reach its conclusion. Britain was highly offended, chastising Wilson for putting their goals on a par with Germany's. Nothing came of the initiative.

America on the Brink:

At the very end of 1916, America was not quite at a critical crossroads, but it was nearing the intersection. A popular, pacifist, cerebral President was re-elected on a platform of having kept the peace without being forced to promise he would continue to do so. Woodrow Wilson knew as well as anyone in America that as long as the bombs were still falling, and u-boats were still prowling, the

United States could still get pulled into the war. Unlike most Americans, who didn't have access to all the confidential casualty figures nor the details on how stockpiles of men and materiel were dwindling rapidly for the Allies, the President was keenly aware that if the war could not be stopped soon, Britain and France, in particular, might be forced to sue for peace. The prospects for a Central Powers victory were chilling and could change the world, and Wilson knew that.

Wilson had done everything he could, by the end of 1916, to force the Central Powers to totally respect America's neutrality. He had only attained mixed results. In truth, the Central Powers, Imperial Germany in particular, could simply not let America off the hook. Under many guises and by many means fair and foul, vital munitions, supplies, foodstuffs, and money were flowing to Germany's enemies from American shores. On top of that, thousands of Americans from dozens of ethnic backgrounds had signed up to fight—were, indeed, fighting—for several different Allied military organizations. It was only a trickle of men, but Germany could only wonder how soon it might turn into a flood, even if they wore the uniforms of other nations than their own.

Only a handful had correctly predicted that the war would become global in scope and last longer than a few months, but they had been right. The implications of the war and also the peace that would result, depending who would emerge victorious, began to weigh heavily on American military and diplomatic strategy. No matter who won, old empires would be changed forever. There would be huge chunks of the globe to be carved up; precious colonies would change hands, old borders would be re-drawn. All of this would create new pressures on American interests and ambitions. Not joining the conflict guaranteed that America would be banned from the bargaining table that forged the peace. The President, and all his senior advisors, were well aware of that—and the possibilities for dire consequences. In short, the United States, as an emerging global power, was between a rock and a very hard place.

Other landmark events that occurred in 1916 included: war pressures brought food rationing in Germany for the first time, a bad omen for the Central Powers' cause; oxycodone was first synthesized in Germany as a pain killer for wounded troops; the composer Gustav Holst released his opus, "The Planets;" and, not surprisingly, the 1916 Olympic Games, scheduled for Berlin, were cancelled.

Nota Bene:

The world saw the passing of the following notables in 1916: William Merritt Chase, the impressionist painter; astronomer Percival Lowell; and, the widely read Jack London, who died at age 40 from a kidney infection.

Notable births in 1916 included: singer Maxine Andrews of the Andrews Sisters; consumer activist Betty Furness; comedian Jackie Gleason; Senator Eugene McCarthy; actor Gregory Peck; violinist Yehudi Menuhin; conductor Robert Shaw; actor Glenn Ford; novelist Harold Robbins; actress Dorothy McGuire; actress Martha Raye; journalist Daniel Schorr; journalist Walter Cronkite; actor Kirk Douglas; and, actress Betty Grable.

⦿ 1916: "He Has Kept Us Out of War" in Photos and Illustrations

A Zeppelin bombs Paris-January

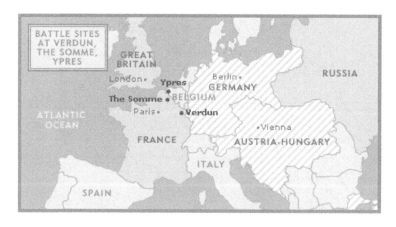

The Battle of Verdun begins-February

A German trench at Verdun...

...and a trench of the French

The battle rages in this contemporary illustration...

...and exacts its toll

Verdun aftermath

French interim cemetery-Verdun

Francisco "Pancho" Villa becomes "America's Most Wanted"-March

Uncle Same declares, "I've had about enough of this."

General Pershing's men chase Villa with all means
at their disposal...

...including technologies old and new

Unrestricted U-boat warfare threatens to cripple
the Allies

U-14 sets out on a patrol-April

Wrigley Field in Chicago begins its storied career,
April 20th

The Marines go marching into Santo Domingo-May
16th

The Saturday Evening Post publishes its first
Norman Rockwell cover-May 20th

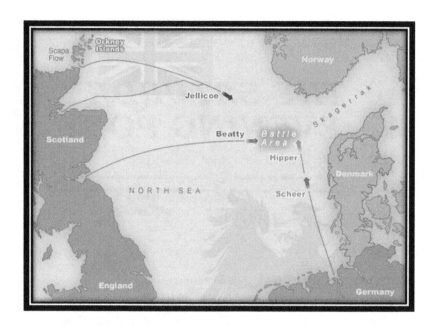

The Battle of Jutland, the largest naval battle of the Great War, takes place May 31st to June 1st off the coast of Denmark

The big guns of the Royal Navy open fire

HMS Invincible explodes and is blown in half during the battle...

...then sinks
Out of a crew of 1,026 there were six survivors

Lithograph of *HMS Warrior* and *HMS Defence* during the battle--both were sunk

Battle damage, *HMS Chester*, punctured by a total of seventeen 150 mm shells during the course of the battle

HMS Chester crewman John Cornwell, age 16, who stood by his gun, though mortally wounded. He received the Victoria Cross, posthumously, for his bravery.

HMS Caroline, a light cruiser, served during the Battle of Jutland...

...and is today permanently moored, as a museum ship, in Belfast, Northern Ireland. She is the last surviving ship from the Battle of Jutland and served the Royal Navy continuously from her commissioning in 1915 to her de-commissioning in 2011.

Famed Justice Louis Brandeis, appointed to the Supreme Court-June 1st

THE AMERICAN WAR–DOG

(The American-German crisis, January–March, 1916)

It was getting harder for President Wilson to ignore
"the barking dog."

HMS Hampshire-1916

Lord Herbert Kitchener ...and as the face of patriotism

The Boy Scouts of America received their Charter-
June 15th

The Berlin Olympics of 1916 were not held because
of the war

The Battle of the Somme commences-July 1st

Life in the trenches-British lines at the Somme

Going "Over the Top..."

...then tending to the wounded...

...on both sides, as British "Tommies" escort
German POW's and wounded

An Irish regiment takes a break from the fighting

British soldiers who have been gassed headed toward the rear for treatment

The tank sees action for the first time at the Somme

A terrible "butcher's bill" would be paid at the Somme by both sides

The true figures can never be known; but, best estimates put British casualties at 420,000; French at 203,000 and German at 465,000. Those killed lie in many cemeteries dedicated to the battle, including the one above.

> MATAWAN, N. J., THURSDAY AFTERNOON, JULY 13, 1916.
>
> # MAN EATING SHARK IN MATAWAN CREEK CAUSES DEATH OF MAN AND BOY
>
> ## W. Stanley Fisher Loses His Life In Trying to Recover Body of Lester Stilwell.
>
> Joseph Dunn, a Brooklyn Boy, Also Attacked and Escapes With Mangled Leg and Foot Made By Shark As He Evidently Was Making His Escape from the Creek— Dynamite and Other Means Used Ineffectually to Find Body of Stilwell Boy.

Was this the inspiration for "Jaws?"

Lester Stillwell
1904- 1916

W. Stanley Fisher
1892 – 1916

The first victims of the great New Jersey shark scare-July

The original Boeing Building, known as "The Big Red Barn"

William Boeing

Schoolgirls march in the San Francisco
Preparedness Parade-July 22nd

Aftermath of the "Black Tom" explosion, Jersey City, NJ, July 30th

The National Park Service and Lassen Volcanic National Park are both created in 1916

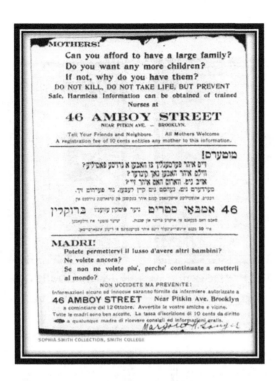

Margaret Sanger's controversial abortion clinic advertisement

Margaret Sanger

The contestants in the 1916 national elections

The President
Woodrow Wilson

The Challenger
Charles Evans Hughes

HMS Britannic, in hospital ship colors

Political cartoon lampooning the u-boat captain that
torpedoed *HMS Britannic*

Tragedy in the Dolomites-December

mountain maneuvers-1916   body found in 1992

A memorial to soldiers lost in the avalanches

⊙ 1917: "For the Rights of Nations Great and Small..."

As the pages of another year turned, the Great War kept grinding on. The war fortunes of both sides waxed and waned; but, for the most part, stalemate was the order of the day. Neither side could engineer any substantial breakthroughs on any of the major fronts, which ran, like ugly scars, all across Europe from the English Channel to the Black Sea. The losses were staggering, far beyond what either side had envisioned in their worst projections. This was especially galling for the Central Powers, led by Germany, who had essentially counted on a "blitzkrieg" type assault to knock either France or Russia—or both—out of the war early. The Kaiser's brain trust knew, going in, that it would be impossible to conduct all-out operations on two fronts for more than a few months; yet, that's exactly what had happened. Russia had proven to be better at waging war than the Germans had planned, and France had been bolstered substantially by Great Britain and her Commonwealth forces. As 1917 began, the Central Powers were being squeezed by a giant nut cracker. Either the pincers would finally crack the "nut" or the nut would prove too hard to break.

The Kaiser and his generals knew, however, that Russia was vulnerable: they could see the seeds of Revolution beginning to sprout and the internal pressures on the Tsar and his government were mounting rapidly. On the other hand, there was America: So far, she had stayed out of it, but there was no doubt that should the United States come in, she would land on the side of the Allies. America, without question, could tip the balance of power.

Germany had one good option, and although not everyone within the Kaiser's government agreed, it was the one she decided to play. The Central Powers would fight a holding action against the Russians, to keep them at bay, while simultaneously taking every division it could spare and hurl it at the Western Front. In addition, the Kreigsmarine would unleash its u-boat force completely, again—no restrictions, no warnings. U-boat commanders were free to torpedo and blast any ship of any nation that might be carrying war supplies to the Allies or helping—as was the Royal Navy—to blockade German ports. The German government knew that unrestricted submarine warfare would likely lead to many more American losses at sea, and a probable declaration of war by the US; but, the Central Powers also believed it would be impossible for the small and weak American Army to build up and deploy a force big enough to make any difference in time to save the Allied cause. Further buoying German hopes was a belief that the American President Wilson, about to embark on his second and final term of office, would not break his promise to keep America out of the war.

1917 in America:

The New Jersey Meadowlands area is, today, the scene of a lot of explosive football action as the NFL Giants and Jets play their home games at MetLife Stadium; but, in 1917 there was a real explosion that even eclipsed the Black Tom debacle of the previous year. In the Meadowlands, then known as Kingsland, a Canadian munitions company had erected an enormous factory to assemble artillery rounds for shipment to Russia. The monthly output at that time was in the vicinity of three million shells, which made the factory a prime target for German saboteurs.

On January 11th, a fire started at the workstation of one Theodore Wozniak, a former enlisted man in the Austrian Army. He had been recruited to the factory by a German national who had obtained the job of employment manager under a false name. Surrounded by open pans of gasoline and gunpowder, the conflagration quickly spread until it consumed half a million artillery shells in spectacular fashion. The factory was leveled. Amazingly, not a single soul was killed, thanks mostly to an alert—and very brave—switchboard operator who stayed at her post phoning every department in the factory warning everyone to flee.

On January 25th, the government of Denmark sold to the United States the Danish West Indies, which promptly became the US Virgin Islands. The price tag was $25 million dollars. The "unincorporated, unorganized territory" of the US consisted of the islands of St. Croix, St. Thomas, and St. John plus the Water Island. The islands were originally discovered by Columbus on his second voyage to the Americas. The tiny cays, islets, and assorted dots of land scattered about the three main islands (supposedly) reminded Columbus of Saint Ursula and her "11,000 virgin hand-maidens;" thus, the "Virgin Islands."

On the same day, another event occurred that certainly had nothing to do with "virgins;" in fact, just the opposite: A huge anti-prostitution rally took place in San Francisco. Some 20,000 people tried to attend an event where there was room for only 7,000. A group of 300 prostitutes addressed the group, pleading their case, saying that poverty had forced them into their trade. When the rally organizer offered to help them find real jobs for $8 to $10 a week, the "ladies" laughed and walked out thereby undermining their cause substantially. As a direct result, the City of San Francisco immediately closed down over 200 known houses of ill repute.

At the end of January, the War Department officially called off the pursuit for Pancho Villa. General Pershing and his troops were ordered back across the border. Pershing was embittered by the experience feeling as if President Wilson had placed too many restrictions on his operations in order to avoid all out war with Mexico. Wilson, for his part, did not want to have a war in his backyard while simultaneously facing the real prospect of being drawn into the much bigger conflict in Europe. Pershing and his men effectively stopped the nasty raids on American territory and bottled up Villa, which was, at least, a tactical victory.

During the month of January, a great debate had taken place among the Kaiser's military men, political leaders, and the admirals in charge of the German Navy. The Kreigsmarine, convinced that unrestricted u-boat warfare could break the supply stranglehold as well as sink munitions headed for the Allies, prevailed in their arguments. Consequently, on January 31st, the German Ambassador to the United States, Count Johann von Bernstorff, presented a note to the US Secretary of State, Robert Lansing, stating unequivocally that Germany would lift all restrictions on u-boat warfare the next day.

This action was tantamount to Germany telling the United States that all bets were off. President Wilson was stunned by the news. Having very little choice, but still not ready to go to war, Wilson went before Congress on February 3rd and announced that the US had severed diplomatic relations with Germany. Wilson left the door to resumption of ties open just a crack: If Germany held back, and respected US ships at sea, despite her declarations, then war might be avoided. Instead, Germany slammed the door shut, sinking several American ships during February and March. In fact, on the very day the US broke off relations with Germany, *U-53* sank the American steamship SS *Housatonic* off the coast of Ireland.

While this was going on, another pot was boiling behind the scenes. The German Foreign Minister, Arthur Zimmerman, sent a secret, coded telegram to Germany's Ambassador to Mexico on January 11th. The Ambassador was to offer up the following to the President of Mexico: should the US declare war on Germany, the Mexican government should declare war on the US and, in turn, the German government would offer monetary and diplomatic support to Mexico to regain most of the territory it had ceded to the United States during the Mexican War of 1848. The British intercepted and decoded the telegram, which they kept to themselves for over a month, fearing that if they revealed it to America, Germany would understand that Britain had cracked their secret codes.

Finally, however, by the end of February, the British were more eager to push the US into the war than protect the secret. The contents of the Zimmerman telegram were forwarded directly to President Wilson on February 24th. The US was relieved to discover that the government of Mexican President Carranza had no interest in the idea, and considered it impractical at best; but, the very idea that Germany would even make the attempt inflamed anti-German feelings. When the text of the telegram and the story was released to the American press on March 3rd, public opinion against the war was impacted to a significant degree: Many Americans were incensed that Germany would help Mexico recover what amounted to the entire states of Texas, Arizona, and New Mexico.

On February 26th, President Wilson asked Congress for the authority to arm US merchant ships and deploy US Navy personnel to man the guns. A last gasp Pacifist effort in the US Senate, undertaken by filibuster, effectively defeated the measure as the Congress adjourned. Wilson's staff dug up an old anti-piracy law allowing the President to take the action anyway via Executive Order. The significance of this measure, other than the obvious, was that placing guns aboard American flag vessels broke the laws of neutrality irrevocably and effectively amounted to a declaration of war.

On March 4th, Woodrow Wilson took the Oath of Office for his second term as President. The public ceremony took place the next day on the windy steps of the East Portico of the Capitol. The temperature was a brisk 38° under cloudy skies. His speech was short, barely 1500 words, and still laced with comments about "peace" and "armed neutrality." His closing comments were hopeful: "The shadows that now lie dark upon our path will soon be dispelled, and we shall walk with the light all about us if we be but true to ourselves—to ourselves as we have wished to be known in the counsels of the world and in the thought of all those who love liberty and justice and the right exalted."

How did America feel at this point? Opinion polling was still in its infancy. Newspapers across the country were widely divided. There was no question, however, that the continuance of Germany's policy on unrestricted submarine warfare, the "Zimmerman Telegram" affair, and actions like the Black Tom and Kingsland bombings were pushing more Americans toward favoring involvement in the war. How many more, or just how many in total were in favor of war, was hard to judge.

The "average American" in 1917 was a factory worker, tradesman, farmer, or homemaker. In the heartlands, far away from both coasts, the European conflict was still remote, little understood, and not of much interest; therefore, a large portion of the population was isolated from the war geographically and emotionally. Attitudes among the "upper classes" were different. Wealthy businessmen tended to be neutral: there was money to be made on war goods, to be sure, but there was also money to be lost, in sinking cargos and overseas loans going bust. Intellectuals were also evenly divided with some seeing the war as a modern crusade and others leery of its moral failings. There was, however, an "elite" group of moneyed men and women, leading families, politicians and high ranking military officers who saw the war as an "assault on democracy." These people, who tended to push a lot of important buttons and pull a great many influential levers, believed that the very fabric of American society was at stake: sooner or later, they believed, if the war wasn't stopped "over there," it would come to the shores of the United Sates.

President Wilson and all his senior advisors believed that if the Central Powers were victorious, the world would be a very different place—and not one friendly to America or democracy in general. The world wide balance of power would shift, and it would not be in favor of the United States. Consequently, on March 20th, the President convened his entire cabinet and polled each of the members on a declaration of war. Every single one of them was in favor.

With great reluctance but a firm resolve, the President told the leaders of Congress he would be coming to address them on April 2nd, seeking a declaration of war against Germany. Against this background was the shocking news that Tsar Nicholas II had abdicated, throwing the Russian government into turmoil. Wilson knew that these events would likely knock Russia out of the war. This, in turn, would free hundreds of thousands of German soldiers for the Western Front. Germany might finally have the ability to deliver the crushing blow long sought against the Allies. Wilson understood clearly that if the Allied cause was to be saved, America would have to do it, and that it was time to do so.

President Wilson made his war request to Congress on April 2nd, barely one month after his second inaugural and only five months after winning his second term on a platform of "peace." The Senate approved the request 82-6 and the House voted in favor 373-50 on April 4th. The first and only female Member of Congress, Jeanette Rankin of Montana, voted "no." America formally declared war on Germany on April 6th. The deed was finally done, and nothing would ever be the same again.

One of Wilson's first decisions after war was declared was to choose the man who would lead America's forces into battle. The leading candidate would surely have been Major General Frederick Funston, who had been Pershing's commander in Mexico. The short, scrappy Funston, nicknamed "Fearless Freddie," had earned a Medal of Honor in the Philippine-American Wars in 1899. He was energetic and well-regarded but a sudden, massive, and fatal heart attack took him out of the picture, at age 51, in February.

The Army Chief of Staff, Major General Hugh Scott was a few months away from mandatory retirement. Former Chief of Staff Major General Leonard Wood coveted the post, but President Wilson distrusted him and disliked him personally — plus he was a staunch Republican who was actually angling for Wilson's job.

Wilson decided to interview Brig. Gen. Pershing, who had acquitted himself well in every assignment he had ever had and was due for some consideration after his service in Mexico. Pershing was offered the job after a brief discussion, and immediately promoted to full General, the first of that rank since Phil Sheridan (who died in office as Commanding General in 1888). Wilson's selection of Pershing proved to be an inspired one, as events would prove.

Former President Roosevelt wanted in on the action, too. He made requests directly to Pershing and Wilson to be commissioned as a Brigadier General and placed in charge of a division. Pershing was in favor, but Wilson politely turned him down citing the danger of the job but privately thinking he didn't need another heroic charge up some foreign hill by a political rival.

With war declared, the martial floodgates opened. America was far from attaining military prowess, but what she did possess was massive reserves of manpower, incredible industrial capacity, and the ability to produce enough food and munitions to equip an army of millions. That was exactly what she would be required to do—and quickly.

The War Department swung into action immediately. The demands for more men and materiel would be staggering. The US Army, by April 1917, consisted of about 200,000 men; 80,000 of whom were in National Guard units scattered across the country. Another 73,000 volunteered immediately; still, more—millions more—would be required. Congress passed a Conscription Act on May 18th and the first draft took place soon thereafter, on June 15th. Before all was said and done, twenty-four million American men would register with their local draft boards. Four and a half million of the registrants would be "called up," with two and half million of those men actually serving, in uniform, before the war's conclusion.

Those who started to swell the rolls would not be the first Americans to fight: young men from the United States had been volunteering to serve since the first days of the war. These soldiers had to join other services, however. The first American to die in combat was a young man from Chicago whose name was Edward Mandell Stone. He was 27 years old, and a graduate of Harvard, Class of 1908. At the war's outset, he was living and working in Paris. He immediately volunteered to serve in the French Foreign Legion. On February 15th, 1915, Mandell, A Soldier 2nd Class, was manning a machine gun near the Aisne battlefield when he was struck by shrapnel and mortally wounded. He died in hospital twelve days later. His family believed he would have wanted to remain in his adopted country and so he rests there still in the French Military Cemetery at Romilly.

Getting Into Gear:

There was no administrative apparatus in place comprehensive enough to coordinate the myriad tasks that would be required to mobilize the men and material needed. Equally daunting, all the soldiers and their equipment had to be readied as fast as humanly possible. Millions of wheels began spinning on the challenges, all without central coordination. As a result, the next twelve months was mass confusion at all levels of government across every area that was needed to support the troops. Capacities were boundless, energies were enormous, enthusiasm was high, but organization was slow in coming.

As a first step, Congress authorized the President to hire up to a million new federal workers to populate five thousand new agencies and boards dedicated to war support. These new bureaucracies spawned mountains of new rules and regulations, all of which would eventually have to be coordinated. Washington had never seen anything quite like this before. Fortunately, the impetus of the Progressive Era, rooted in the former Roosevelt administration, was still in vogue: Progressives valued the virtues of hard work, modernization, and efficiency; therefore, although confusing at first, the gears soon began to mesh more smoothly. The new army of bureaucrats attacked each major task with enthusiasm and grit.

Manpower:

With attitudes about the war among the general population uncertain, Wilson and his advisors went immediately to all-out conscription to raise an army large enough to matter. This was the first time a mass draft had been held since the Civil War and the Administration was intent on avoiding the mistakes of that near fiasco. In the first go-around, all males 21 to 31 (expanded soon after to 18 to 45) were required to register. Exemptions would be given for those found not physically fit, engaged in what were determined to be essential occupations, those with family dependencies, and men who objected on verifiable religious grounds. There would be no "bounty system," as had existed during the Civil War, whereby a draft eligible man could pay a substitute to serve for him. Local draft boards were established consisting of an area's leading citizens, who, in turn, would be responsible for local quotas and the actual drafting of specific men. The War Department was given authority to go after those who either resisted the draft (approximately 487,000 of 24 million eligible men) or willfully deserted after being drafted (approximately 174,000 out of nearly 3 million actually conscripted). Those who tried in one way or another to avoid their obligation were derisively known as "slackers."

Although there was no massive wave of volunteers after war was declared, the eligible male population of the country generally lined up willingly to register. This was an era when "duty and honor" still resonated: In fact, a national poll taken after the war found that among the men who served and fought, there was no real bitterness or dissatisfaction with having answered the call. The

157

vast majority said that they believed it was their moral obligation to serve and were proud to have done so.

The man upon whose shoulders most of the responsibility would fall was Secretary of War Newton D. Baker, Jr. There was hardly a more unlikely candidate: Rail thin, barely over five feet tall, Baker had volunteered for duty in the Spanish-American War but had been rejected for poor eyesight. He was an avowed Pacifist with no training in military matters whatsoever. Yet, before his term as Secretary was over (1921), he would be in charge of one of the world's most powerful armed forces and one of the planet's largest bureaucracies. When offered the assignment he told reporters, "I do not know anything about this job."

He didn't need to: he was a friend and confidant of the President. They had met when both were at Johns Hopkins University in the 1890's. Wilson went on to be President of Princeton and Governor of New Jersey before becoming President of the United States. Baker went on to be a successful lawyer and Mayor of Cleveland, Ohio (1912-15). Baker had also been very involved in Wilson's presidential campaign and was twice offered the job of Secretary of the Interior, which he declined both times. When Wilson's first Secretary of War, Lindley Garrison, became a little too bellicose, the two had a falling out, and Garrison resigned. Wilson felt his pacifist friend

Baker would be the right replacement. He also wanted Baker's sharp legal mind applied to some of the challenges facing the War Department in Mexico, the Philippines, and Europe. Baker ultimately proved to be an excellent choice.

Baker was not cowed in the least by the be-medaled chests and brass buttons all around him. He was a compromiser who tried to ascertain the heart of any issue then find the best path to a solution. He inherited a department totally unprepared for the challenges it faced and in a remarkably short period of time he turned it into an efficiently functioning operation.

Knowing he could not do it all himself, his first challenge centered on finding the right people to assist him; men whom he could trust to be given the authority they needed, then do the job. Pershing would be his point man and field commander. Baker told him: "I will give you only two orders, one to go to France and the other to come home. In the meantime, your authority in France will be supreme." Baker was smart enough to understand that there was no way he or any other Washingtonian could run the fight from across the Atlantic. If it was going to be a successful venture, he needed to trust the man in charge, and he did.

What Baker could do was make sure that Pershing and his men had everything they could possibly need and the maximum in support and coordination from the home front. As an example of the chaos then abounding, Baker found, by July, that there were already in place one hundred and fifty separate purchasing committees, often competing for the same goods; worse, some committees hoarded supplies other committees needed to meet their needs. The War Department was, in essence, often competing against itself.

The Army's governing body, the General Staff, was a small operation limited by regulation to less than twenty general officers and their various lower ranking aides. There was far too much work for such a small organization and, as the war commenced, most of the truly competent senior officers were being siphoned off for important field and training commands. Baker would have to expand the General Staff rapidly as well as better distribute its critical functions. To help, Baker made three crucial (and excellent) appointments.

Baker hired, as Assistant Secretary of War, an experienced industrialist by the name of Benedict Crowell. Baker had known Crowell, a Yale graduate and PhD, in Cleveland where Crowell had been a leading executive in several steel and mining companies. Crowell was a Major in the Army Reserve (who rose to Brigadier General) with experience in artillery and munitions. He was also considered one of the leading efficiency experts of his day. In addition to his job as Assistant

Secretary, Baker placed Crowell directly in charge of the Munitions Board.

To untangle the mess that Army supply had become, Baker called out of retirement Major General George Washington Goethals, the man who had successfully completed the Panama Canal. If anyone could made sense of the Quartermaster Corps, it would be the man who had snatched victory from the jaws of the potential disaster the Canal had nearly become.

After the aging caretaker Chiefs of Staff respectfully completed their retirements (Major General Hugh Scott in September and Major General Tasker Bliss the following May), Baker was free to choose someone young, energetic and talented to assume the role as the Army's head. He picked Major General Peyton March, 53, a West Point graduate and accomplished artillery officer. March set about successfully reorganizing the Army's entire command structure and revamping the standards for a modern 20th Century Chief of Staff's role.

Sitting at the same table during Cabinet meetings was the Secretary of War's counterpart, Josephus Daniels, the powerful Secretary of the Navy. Today, the various service secretaries (Army, Navy, and Air Force) are subordinate to the Secretary of Defense, a new Cabinet position created in 1947; but in Wilson's day, the Secretary of the Navy was equal in rank to the Secretary of War.

Daniels was a lawyer by training but a newspaperman by trade, and before his appointment, the long-time publisher of the Raleigh, North Carolina, *News and Observer*. A strong supporter of Democratic causes (and white supremacy), he was very instrumental in garnering support in the South for Wilson's run for President. As a reward, he received the post as Secretary of the Navy. Like Baker, he had no experience whatsoever in military matters. Daniels appointed, as his principal assistant, an energetic and talented young subordinate by the name of Franklin D. Roosevelt.

Daniels, who had a moralistic streak reflecting Wilson's own prudish ways, banned alcohol from US Navy ships in 1914. It was not a popular move among the sailors. Coffee and grape juice became the common substitutes and the term "a cup of joe" derisively referred to Daniels ban on spirits. Likewise, in 1917, he banned houses of prostitution within five miles of any active naval base. This, too, had a deleterious effect on naval morale to say nothing of the relocation of numerous "businesses" scattered across the naval landscape.

Secretary Daniels was expert at handling the politics and social responsibilities of his office—and advocating for the Navy. He wisely left most of the hard work on procurement and ship building to Roosevelt, who had long harbored a fascination with and fondness for all things naval. Of the two major services, the Army and the Navy, the Navy was better prepared when war broke out; but, in reality, there was still a lot of catching up to do to place the US Navy on the same competitive level as the world's best fleets (Britain, France, Germany, Italy, and Japan).

The US Navy, on the brink of WW I, consisted of an aging, coal-fired battleship fleet that was short on destroyers and submarines. It was also hide-bound to the concept of the "big gun" and engaging in pitched battles at sea among monstrously large ships. There was no room for the type of strategic thinking placing the u-boat or the submarine at the center of the action, as was taking place in Germany and rattling the nerves of the Royal Navy. Aviation and aircraft carriers weren't even considered serious prospects; in fact, Admiral William Benson, the Chief of Naval Operations in 1916 was quoted as saying, "I cannot conceive of any use the fleet will ever have for aviation."

Many of the twenty-three pre-dreadnaught battleships in the 1917 inventory had taken part in the "Great White Fleet" around-the-world cruise initiated by President Roosevelt in 1908. Although the US Navy, and a whole generation of its junior officers and career sailors had gained enormous practical experience during this exercise, by 1917 they were manning the outdated equipment of a previous era. The navies of the major combatants in the Great War had far outstripped the US Navy in ship size, speed, propulsion, and firepower by the start of the war. The stance of the pre-war US Congress and the Navy's own Secretary had done little to build up the Navy's capability, relying on a pacifist nation's desires to maintain the peace.

By 1916, things began to change. The *Lusitania* sinking and the mounting losses being sustained by the allied navies because of u-boat warfare opened many eyes. The Navy began to worry about the possibility of the Royal Navy being swept from the seas and German u-boats patrolling brazenly off the Atlantic Coast of America. An expanded Navy was seen as a much needed defensive force, not solely as a response to jingoistic war aims. As a result, Congress passed the Naval Act of 1916 which became known as "the Big Navy Act."

Although the law, and its appropriations, would be altered substantially as the war evolved, this was a huge boost for the Navy. The Act authorized the construction of ten big, oil fired battleships, six battlecruisers, ten scout cruisers, fifty destroyers, thirty submarines, and a host of smaller auxiliary ships. When President Wilson was told the Act would make the US Navy bigger and better than Britain's in three years he boasted, "Let us build a navy bigger than hers and do what we please."

Luckily for the US Navy, the Chief Constructor at the time was the remarkable Rear Admiral David W. Taylor. A brilliant engineer and naval architect, Taylor had graduated first in his class at the US Naval Academy in 1885. While there, he set an academic achievement record that still stands today. He was commissioned as an Assistant Naval Constructor in 1886. In 1888 he was sent to the Royal Naval College in Greenwich, England, where he once again achieved the highest academic grades ever recorded in that school. By 1914 he had been made rear admiral and Chief of the Bureau of Naval Construction and Repair. It would be Taylor's job to turn the "Big Navy Act" into ships.

The task ahead of Taylor and his Bureau was to make the US Navy "second to none." The battleships contemplated would be "super-dreadnaughts" with the thickest armor, biggest guns, and most powerful engines Taylor could put in their hulls. To complement the big battle wagons, an entirely new class of ship, the battlecruiser, was approved. These quasi-battleships would have the big guns, but they would be lighter and faster. It would be the job of the battlecruiser to sweep away any ship less powerful than itself and yet be able to run away from any ship more powerful, leaving the "heavy lifting" to the super dreadnaughts.

To assist in the design and construction of these new ships, the Royal Navy sent one their experts to Taylor who had dissected the structural failures that had doomed the *Titanic*. They also let Taylor borrow several naval architects who had assisted in the design of Britain's newest heavy battleships. Britain had just fought the Battle of Jutland and although the outcome was debated, it had seemed to have proven the need for large caliber weapons to defend the fleet as well as keep the enemy bottled up and ineffective. The advocates for the "Big Gun" Navy were in their heyday—then everything changed, almost overnight.

The rise to prominence of the u-boat and unrestricted submarine warfare swept the battleship blueprints off the drawing boards. Battleships were virtually useless against submarines and incapable of escorting merchant convoys: neither could they haul large numbers of troops or pack away the vast stores of supplies that would be needed to support the men.

Taylor was forced to take the manpower, shipyards, and new appropriations and turn the construction effort into destroyers to hunt the u-boats, auxiliaries to haul the men and munitions, and submarines for the Navy's own undersea campaigns. Almost all the battleships would be abandoned and none of the radical battlecruisers would ever be finished (although two would be repurposed into the Navy's first keel-up aircraft carriers). It was a monumental challenge and it was fortunate that the US Navy had an engineering genius like Taylor to mastermind the process.

The "Doughboys" March Off to War:

The etymology of the term "Doughboy" is somewhat obscure: It was in common use as far back as the 1848-50 Mexican War and could have referred to either the fried dough concoctions that the soldiers in the field prepared for themselves or the way they looked—all covered in "dough" flour—after a long day's march through the dry, dusty arroyos of Mexico. In any case, the term popped up again, mostly among the troops themselves, as they shipped out to one of the thirty-two massive camps, or cantonments, that the US Army set up to train the millions that would be required. The sites were scattered around the country and whether they called themselves "Doughboys," "Yanks," or "Sammies" (for Uncle Sam), they would be in training for a required sixteen weeks.

During that period of time, the cowhands, bakers, farmers, mechanics, accountants and ordinary citizens of all stripes and sizes, those who had made it through the initial rounds of the draft, would be homogenized into the initial one million fighting men Pershing said he would need by the end of 1918. The tens of thousands of officers necessary to lead these men would come out of separate officer training programs. Many of the necessary lieutenants and captains, even a few majors, would come from the former Plattsburgh

Campers who had been preparing themselves for leadership roles since 1915. "Ninety-day wonder" programs (the time allocated to train and commission an officer) sprang up at colleges and universities all across the land. Even given the nightmarish, confusing, contradictory, and frustrating procurement and equipment problems, the massive giant slowly worked itself up to its potential and the troops poured out of their camps, ready to go "over there."

The first troops to go to France actually left soon after the declaration of war. The President, General Pershing, and Secretary Baker all felt that at least a token presence was required: It would show, at the very least, that America was finally committed to the cause and ready to go into action. The challenge was, of course, that very few troops were truly ready. The first troops to head overseas were members, appropriately, of the 1st Division. The division would consist of two brigades of two regiments each, about 17,000 men in all, 11,000 of them infantrymen. Even this token force depleted the Regular Army to near zero, with the balance sent out to form the nuclei of other divisions in formation.

The "Big Red One," as the division became known, with a distinctive shoulder patch to match, started sailing for France on June 14th. By agreement with their allied partners, the Americans would be encamped near Lorraine, about 120 miles southwest of Paris. The area was one of the more quiet sectors on the Western Front and it would give the Yanks time to train and organize their forces.

On July 4th, after being persuaded by the French, Pershing allowed the 2nd Battalion of the 16th Infantry to march through the streets of Paris to celebrate America's Independence Day. It turned out to be a brilliant move that helped boost the dispirited people of "The City of Light." The parade concluded at Lafayette's tomb where Quartermaster Colonel Charles E. Stanton offered up a rousing oration in fluent French, further animating the crowd. He concluded with the famous words (often attributed incorrectly to Pershing), "Lafayette! We are here!"

The Marquis would have been proud, no doubt, but there was still much work ahead. Both the British and the French had immediate designs on the deployment of the fresh American forces. The British plan was the more ambitious one—and the least palatable to President Wilson and General Pershing. The British proposed what they termed "amalgamation;" or, simply assimilating American troops into British units led by British officers. The French were willing to keep American units whole and segregated, but wanted to feed them into the trenches alongside French units.

To the immense credit of American leadership, amalgamation was rejected outright. Pershing, for one, believed it would diminish the visibility of the American contribution and that he and the other American officers would simply lose control of their portion of the conflict. Likewise, the French plan was politely rejected: Pershing wanted responsibility for an "American sector" along the front, so that he and his subordinates could maintain responsibility for their own fate. Britain and France backed down—for the time being. Pershing was assigned a portion of the Lorraine sector and he and his staff dug in and began preparing for combat.

The Weapons:

In the history of American combat arms, there has hardly been a more rugged, reliable, or successful infantry weapon than the Model 1903 Springfield rifle. First designed and manufactured by the famous Springfield (Massachusetts) Armory in 1903, this .30 caliber rifle had a service life that lasted until the Vietnam War. The "ought-three" weighed a little under nine pounds, had a twenty-four inch barrel, accommodated a five-round clip, and could fire accurately out to almost 3,000 feet. There were minor quibbles about the front and rear sights and the initial bayonet was deemed too fragile, but the rifle experienced very few failures even under combat conditions and the mud-filled trenches.

At the start of the American troop exodus to France, the Springfield and Rock Island (Illinois) Arsenals had produced nearly a million Model 1903 rifles already and production of another one million was stepped up. The Doughboys also had the Lee-Enfield rifle available: This weapon was the standard infantry rifle for the British and all the Commonwealth armies. It weighed about the same, was slightly longer, and fired similar ammunition. The Royal Arsenals and commercial manufacturers of the Lee-Enfield started making a version that would use the Model 1903 ammunition as soon as the Americans entered the war, thus making many more rifles available to the US troops—and standardizing their ammunition.

Heavier weapons were more problematic. The US Army was short on automatic weapons, especially machine guns, at the start of WW I. The Army had used the Gatling gun, first manufactured in the Civil War, right up through the Spanish-American War. In the years prior to the Great War, the Army was still experimenting with various models and did not have a large inventory of any one type. As a result, as the American involvement ramped up, the Yanks were forced to start hostilities with several Allied models, primarily the French Model 1915 Chauchat and the Model 1909 Benet-Mercie. The popular and effective Browning Automatic Rifles (BAR's), made specifically for the American forces, would not debut in action until early 1918.

The state of American field artillery at the commencement of hostilities was even worse. The US Army had in inventory about six hundred 3-inch field pieces, mostly the Model 1902 type. Only about one hundred of these guns made it to France: The balance were kept stateside for training purposes. American artillery units would rely on the French made 75-mm field piece. France gave the Yanks nearly 4, 000 of these guns and ten million rounds of ammunition. These pieces formed the backbone of American artillery operations for the duration.

At the start of the conflict, the entire air arm was in very poor shape. The Signal Corps had been in charge of air operations since 1914 and had done little to strengthen the service. When the Army Air Service came into being as a separate force in 1917, air capability began to improve rapidly; still, over the course of America's involvement, over three-quarters of the aircraft flown by American pilots were made in either France or Britain. [Note: A full chapter on the American Expeditionary Force's Air Operations will follow.]

Vice Admiral William Sims was the senior US Navy representative in London, having been sent there by President Wilson in early 1917. Sims was a gunnery expert of long standing, former battleship commander, and most recently President of the prestigious Naval War College. As he looked over the forces he would soon be leading into combat, as the new Commander, Naval Forces Europe, he was dismayed. He later declared (after the war) that only ten percent of the Navy's ships were fully manned, the rest lacked up to forty percent of their required crews, and, in his opinion, only a third of the ships were ready for war.

It was clear that whatever the US Navy could contribute to the war effort would be expended primarily in the Atlantic, where the conflict was focused. It also became apparent very early on that the order of battle the US Navy possessed was inadequate to do the job.

The US Navy could send to war twenty three out-dated pre-dreadnaught battleships along with ten newer battleships, fifty destroyers, thirty-four cruisers, twenty three torpedo boats (small destroyers), eighteen submarines, and a handful of auxiliaries, including just sixteen transport ships.

"Beans and Bullets:"

A couple of million men needed to be armed, clothed, equipped—and fed. At the beginning of America's participation in the Great War there was no organizational structure in place to do any of this. As noted above, hundreds of competing boards and committees sprang into being, and not all of them with the most patriotic or altruistic of intentions: There was money to be made, and smart American businessmen began circling like sharks around the blood in the water.

No one knew, of course, that the Great War was only going to last another eighteen months. It had already gone on far longer than most had imagined, but there were still no mile markers in sight that would signal the end of the journey. Even General Pershing was making plans for deploying new divisions into the American sector through the end of 1919 when he expected to have two million men, and maybe as many as one hundred divisions in France. The plans for supply that were being put in place anticipated several more years of struggle—and potential profit.

From all this chaos emerged a remarkable organization that came to be known as the War Industries Board. This military-civilian group had come into being via the 1916 National Defense Act, passed by a Congress that was beginning to believe that war was inevitable and that something had better be done to prepare American industry for it. The 1916 Act had created the Council of National Defense, the governing body for plans and policies under the Act. The Council, in turn, created the Munitions Standards Board as one of its constituent entities and placed it in charge of standardizing all munitions production and getting the necessary American companies tooled up to produce the bullets and other ordnance that would be needed. It soon became apparent, however, that the vast needs for materiel across a wide number of industries would require more than just making bullets: the Munitions Board morphed into the much more powerful War Industries Board.

It's hard to imagine, today, just how much power and control this seven member group had over American industry during its brief existence. The WIB had the ability to set quotas, demand standardization among competing factories, allocate natural resources, and even settle strikes by controlling wages. For most of its tenure the WIB was led by the self-made multi-millionaire of Wall Street fame, Bernard M. Baruch. He was extraordinarily good at his job, so much so, in fact, that after the Great War, even though a civilian, he was awarded the Army's Distinguished Service Medal.

Under the WIB, American industrial efficiency increased dramatically and supply problems for the war effort began to subside. Naturally, it took many months for all the changes to be implemented; and, in truth, much of what the Board accomplished in terms of production proved to be unnecessary, as the war ended sooner than most anticipated. Nonetheless, huge fortunes were also made amidst the speculation. Federal examinations of some of these windfalls actually carried on until the mid 1930's.

The Army's representative on the WIB was Brigadier General Hugh Johnson—the youngest Brigadier General in the US Army since the Civil War. He was just 37. He had graduated from West Point in 1903 (with Douglas MacArthur) and had seen service in the Philippines and as Superintendent of Sequoia National Park when the US Army controlled national park properties. He went to law school, joined the Judge Advocate

General's Corps, served with Pershing in Mexico, helped write the Selective Service Act of 1917, and then became instrumental in conducting the first draft. He was ornery, combative, and difficult to work with; but, Bernard Baruch liked him and his abilities, and that's all the patronage Johnson needed.

The Navy's representative on the WIB was Rear Admiral Frank F. Fletcher, a Naval Academy graduate, Class of 1875, and Medal of Honor awardee for his participation in the 1914 Vera Cruz conflict. He was a former head of Navy material and an experienced battleship commander. For his service on the WIB he was further awarded both the Navy and Army Distinguished Service Medals before retiring in 1919.

The uniforms that the Doughboys went off to war clothed in were based on the British tunic design. They were also an attempt to combine utility with comfort and uniformity. The Army had started recognizing the need for uniforms that fit the climate during the Spanish-American War. It was also about this time that double stitching came into vogue (for durability) as well as removable buttons (for ease of laundering and cleaning). Khaki cotton would be the standard for summer wear and olive drab wool for winter. The only difference between officer and enlisted uniforms were rank insignia and a black band at the cuff of an officer's sleeve. Campaign and garrison caps were issued to all ranks, and brown 48-eye boots were standard, along with puttees. The use of dress uniforms was suspended for the duration, as their use in and around the trenches were deemed impractical, at best.

The Quartermaster Corps was seriously deficient in the numbers of uniforms required at the start of the conflict. Many American uniforms were actually manufactured in England and France and caught up with some of the troops as they got off the transports.

Naval uniforms had not changed much since the 1880's, and officer uniforms were entirely distinct from enlisted "blue jackets." Officers wore high-collared tunics with hidden buttons and gold stripes on their sleeves depicting their various ranks. Enlisted sailors wore the ubiquitous jumpers or "blouses," and the famous bell-bottom pants. Navy blue was the color for all ranks in cold weather and white for the warmer months. Not much would change for the Navy until long after the war concluded.

The WW I Doughboy probably ate better than any field soldier in history, even better than his contemporary allies. The Quartermaster Corps was responsible for feeding the men in the field. By any standard of the day, they did a remarkable job.

The interior lines of the Americans were much shorter than the French or British, so that made things a bit easier for supply and food delivery. The US Army had access to rail lines for their exclusive use, bringing fresh supplies directly from their debarkation ports. The roads across the American front, in general, were well maintained by the Corps of Engineers.

Trench duty was horrible, to say the least, and a real morale problem. Cooking in the trenches was nearly impossible with the constant dirt, mud, filth and vermin—to say nothing of the bombs, bullets and artillery. The Quartermasters decided that, whenever and wherever possible, they would prepare hot food behind the lines, then send it up to the boys at the front. Tremendous innovations were made in field kitchens in France, including new-design tins, food containers, buckets, and wagons that made the delivery of hot food from remote kitchens possible. The Doughboys even had real dough: the Quartermaster Corps set up and operated dozens of field bakeries during the war. The difference was profound between hot bread and warm biscuits versus hardtack crackers or stale bread from a can.

The delivery of hot food was not always possible, of course. When the men in the field were forced to rely on pre-prepared rations, or packaged food, they had four choices. First, there was an item dubbed the "Iron Ration," which had actually been around since 1907. This stark, sealed, tin packet held three, 3-ounce "cakes" made of beef bouillon and pre-cooked parched wheat, plus salt and pepper packets. "Dessert" was three, 1-ounce pieces of sweet chocolate. The Iron

Ration was intended primarily as an emergency meal, and from its description there is little wonder as to why that was so.

Second, soldiers could avail themselves of the "Trench Ration." These were commercially produced under government contract and shipped in large, heavy cases meant to be broken open in the field. Each tin-covered box came wrapped in canvas. Inside each case were a number of canned meats, including salmon, pork and beans, corned beef, sardines, etc.. Most soldiers pronounced them "edible," but the large packing cases were difficult to lug around the trenches.

As the war progressed, a third choice emerged, that being the so-called "Reserve Ration." This item was packaged for the individual Doughboy and held either 12 ounces of fresh bacon or one pound of canned meat, usually corned beef. Also included were two cans, one each, of hardtack and hard bread; plus, packets of pre-ground coffee, sugar, and salt. Finally, there was a packet containing a tobacco ration: a half ounce of cut tobacco and ten cigarette rolling papers (soon replaced by machine-made cigarettes).

Notice, in all of these choices, there is no mention of fresh fruit and vegetables or even canned varieties. These "delicacies," when available, were delivered on an ad hoc basis and issued as separate items. On many occasions they were only issued when some enterprising Sammie "liberated" a case of canned peaches for his squad mates.

The fourth option was, by far, the best, as far as each soldier was concerned: the packet from home. These "care packages" were not only a huge boost in morale, but often the only source of anything remotely resembling "real food." Unfortunately for the men at the front, the US Postal Service and the Army's postal service took many months to get coordinated. It wasn't, in fact, until May of 1918 that the mail coming to the troops was finally placed under Army control, at which point, delivery became smoother and more timely. There were a number of amusing and apocryphal examples of food packages travelling through the postal system to the front: One caring mother sent her son six fresh bananas which were literally unrecognizable by the time they got to France. Another wife sent her husband a loaf of fresh bread every day—the first loaf arriving three months after it was shipped. One officer was sent either a jar of pickles or preserves every day: he received the first five dozen jars on the same day.

"The First to Fight:"

By late June, the Americans were in France at division strength—the venerable First Division— and all divisions, as operating units, were going to be at force levels that enfolded about 25,000 men. This was, of course, a token force; the precursor to what Pershing and his allied partners were expecting to grow to about a million men by the end of 1918.

Even at token levels, the impact was profound: the Germans certainly knew they were going to be facing a serious manpower challenge once the American infusions got up-to-speed. Any plans they had to push toward a rapid conclusion of the war, in their favor, would have to be accelerated before the American contingent became too sizeable to overcome. The Allies—France and Britain—were buoyed immeasurably by the small contingent of Americans that boiled off the transport ships at St. Nazaire: morale among their battered troops soared.

The eager, amiable, laughing, rollicking, Yanks were finally in France, but they were far from ready to enter the trenches. There was a tremendous amount of training to be done to get the troops in fighting form, and that was the primary task facing Pershing and his staff. Pershing, in fact, didn't even want his men in the trenches. He knew, of course, that trench warfare would be inevitable, due to that war's very nature, but he was unwilling to commit his men to that method of combat alone. He wanted his soldiers to train to fight in the open as well. Pershing was unwilling to accept the mindset that had taken hold of the war leaders of both sides, that of fighting yard by yard, trench by trench. He wanted to attack, attack, attack across open ground, devouring large tracts of land, breaking the lines and moving ahead. It would certainly not be possible in each and every situation, but Pershing felt mobility was the best use of his forces, and he planned accordingly.

He also steadfastly refused to break his units into smaller cohorts and feed them piecemeal into the lines with his allies. The Americans would fight as one, alongside their partners, but not as part of someone else's army. The only concession he made along these lines—a wise one—was to have entire divisions, regiments, or brigades train alongside equally sized units of their more experienced partners, especially the French.

After two months of intense shuffling, prodding and planning, Pershing's basic staff and command structure was in place. To signify both his firm resolve to keep the AEF independent, as well as to get his troops in position for their first moves against the enemy in their assigned sector (Lorraine), Pershing moved his entire headquarters, in September, to Chaumont, about one hundred twenty five miles southeast of Paris. This set him up along the Marne River, with good interior lines and direct routing along good roads—and railroads—from the primary point of debarkation and supply from the port of St. Nazaire.

By late September-early October, Pershing had four divisions in France, over 100,000 men. The 1st Division was joined by the 2nd, which, unlike any other so far, had a brigade of US Marines, led by Major General John LeJeune. Also arriving was the 26th Division, made up mostly of National Guard units from New England, and the 42nd "Rainbow Division," so-called because it consisted of units from a myriad of States. One hundred thousand men may have seemed, to some, an enormous number, but in the war these men were joining, the loss of half that number in a single battle was an all-too-common occurrence.

Divisions arrived in uniform, each man with a standard kit and the few personal items permitted. Each soldier had been through the prescribed weeks of basic training, but they were still unprepared for war. Very few—almost none— had received any of the advanced training that would be required to prepare them for the realities of that war. All divisions, after landing, would begin three to four months of additional training in areas such as hand grenades, mortar operation, demolitions, and chemical warfare. Machine gunners and artillerymen were introduced to their new weapons, most of them of French manufacture. Last but not least, at Pershing's insistence, all infantrymen underwent advanced training in open field marksmanship and use of the bayonet: the troops were going to get up and out of the detested trenches if Pershing had anything to say in the matter.

By late October, Pershing was willing to cautiously test the waters and allowed the 1st

Division to send in one regiment at a time to spend ten days alongside an equivalent French regiment. On November 3, 1917, the 16th Infantry—the very same unit that General Pershing had allowed to symbolically march through the streets of Paris in June—was stationed near Artois. A French deserter informed the Germans that the Americans were in the lines opposite their position. The Germans were eager to test both the mettle of their new foes as well as learn as much about their dispositions and equipment as possible. They decided to stage a trench raid to capture prisoners and equipment. Company F of the 116th became the unwitting foils of the German intelligence mission.

At a little after 0230, a force of about 200 stormed across the no-man's land between the German and American trenches. The surprised Americans quickly found themselves overwhelmed and in a hand-to-hand fight. They rallied and beat the enemy back, but not before the Germans could escape with twelve prisoners and armloads of gear and equipment. They also left behind five wounded and three dead Yanks. No one knows who died first, but three young soldiers became the first American combat casualties of the war. They were: Corporal James Bethel Gresham, Private Thomas Enright and Private Merle D. Hay.

James B. Gresham was a factory worker from Evansville, Indiana, who had enlisted in the Army in 1914. He had been born in Kentucky in 1893. At the time of his death he was a squad leader in Company F. His bravery during this battle earned him a posthumous Silver Star as well as a Purple Heart. He was initially buried on the battlefield, but later moved to the American Cemetery in Bathlemon, France. Ultimately, though, his family wanted him home; so, in 1921, his remains were returned to Indiana, which is where he rests today.

Thomas Francis Enright, born in Pittsburgh, Pennsylvania, May 8, 1887, was from Irish stock, his parents having immigrated to the United States. He had enlisted in the Army in 1909. He, too, was from Company F and like CPL Gresham, buried on the field of honor. In a somewhat bizarre twist, it was said that alfalfa soon sprouted from the soil above the graves, and that Enright's family harvested some of it, and baked a loaf of bread with the grain and ate it in Enright's honor. Enright's remains were later returned home to Pittsburgh, and he had a hero's funeral, complete with a wreath sent by General Pershing.

Merle David Hay was an Iowa boy and farm store clerk, born in 1896. As soon as the first call for volunteers was raised in 1917, Hay signed up. After initial training at Ft. Bliss, Texas, he was off to France in June. Also with Company F, Hay was seen with a bayonet in one hand and a pistol in the other, struggling with two German soldiers before he went down with a single pistol shot to the head. Buried with his comrades, he, too, was ultimately returned to the United States and reburied with full military honors in Iowa in 1921.

And so, the first American blood had been shed, but there would be much more.

The End of the Beginning:

As 1917 waned, prospects for the Allies were about as bleak as they had ever been, while the hopes of the Central Powers were being renewed. Russia's armed forces had all but withdrawn from the conflict amidst governmental turmoil and revolution. The Czar had abdicated and he and his immediate family had been placed in custodial exile inside Russia. The collapse of Russia's war effort freed dozens of German divisions for duty on other fronts. A combined Austrian-German force had routed the Italians by late October and effectively eliminated them from the war. That left just one other front—the Western—for Germany and her partners to deal with, and they turned in that direction with a renewed vigor. Even though the German populace was near starvation, the government all but bankrupt, and new recruits to replace losses non-existent, the German high command was exuberant. They believed the Allies were on the ropes, that the Americans couldn't possibly get prepared in time to become a factor, and that one final all-out push would win the war.

They were not far wrong. Britain and France were experiencing the same kinds of manpower shortages experienced by the Central Powers. U-boat warfare was having a devastating effect on Allied supplies. The French Army, after crushing losses earlier in the year, especially during the Nivelle Offensive, where over 118,000 Frenchmen became casualties, mutinied. Half the French divisions along the Western Front told their commanders that they would no longer participate in offensive operations—especially the suicidal full-frontal charges that had been all too common. They would repel attacks, but they would not advance.

The situation with the British was not much better: The Passchendaele Campaign, engineered by the British commander General Sir Douglas Haig, which ran from April to November, ended badly and cost the British over 200,000 casualties. Prime Minister David Lloyd George, who had never favored the campaign, was so gob smacked by the losses that he withheld replacements so that Haig would have to stay on the defensive.

The Allies, out of desperation, turned to Pershing, begging him to speed up the insertion of American troops into the lines. There was new talk of "amalgamation;" or, integrating American units into the depleted units of both France and Britain. Amalgamation talks reached all the way to the War Department and the White House but Secretary Baker and President Wilson kicked the can right back to Pershing who remained adamant that American units would fight together under their own officers.

Pershing was not simply being stubborn: he knew the realities, but he and his senior officers firmly believed that Germany was also on the ropes and that the Allies, though fatigued, were probably not as desperate as they, themselves, feared. Pershing personally favored withholding the bulk of the American forces—present and on the way—for total deployment until 1919. On this, however, he did bend, and the early months of 1918 would see the first substantial American forays into combat.

Meanwhile, the Germans were sharpening their knives once more and began planning a series of ambitious early spring 1918 offensives. With these complexities and realities, 1917 came to an end.

◉ 1917: "For the Rights of Nations Great and Small..." in Photos and Illustrations

The Kingsland Explosion in the Meadowlands, New Jersey-scattered shells lay everywhere-January 11th

The US Virgin Islands were acquired from Denmark-January 25th

A contemporary poster occasioned by the torpedoing of the American steamship *SS Housatonic* on February 3rd.

Kaiser Wilhelm II (C) and his senior advisors, Gen. Paul von Hindenburg (L), Chief of Staff, and Gen. Erich Ludendorff (R) plot strategy-February-1917.

The "Zimmerman Telegram" offered Arizona, New Mexico and Texas to Mexico if there was a declaration of war against the United States-February.

President Wilson authorized the arming of merchant ships with US Navy guns and gun crews, such as these sailors and their 3"-inch naval rifle-February 26[th.]

President Wilson's 2nd Inaugural-March 4th

President Wilson went before Congress to request a
Declaration of War-April 2nd

The New York Times announced the war declaration with
banner headlines-April 3rd

Maj. Gen. Frederic "Fearless Freddie" Funston, Medal of Honor awardee, who would have commanded the American Expeditionary Force save for a fatal heart attack, age 51, February 19[th.]

General John J. "Black Jack" Pershing (1860-1948), the man who did get the assignment

Edward Mandell Stone, Harvard Class of 1908, The first American to die in the Great War, as a Soldier 2nd Class, French Foreign Legion, Romilly, France, February 27th, 1915.

Men started registering for conscription-June

Secretary of War Newton D. Baker-the man who would bear the burden of preparing America for war and sending millions of "Doughboys" to France.

Josephus Daniels, Secretary of the Navy, 1913-1921

Franklin D. Roosevelt, Asst. Secretary of the Navy,
1913-1920

Secretary Daniels did away with the Navy's "rum ration"
and banned alcohol aboard all US Navy ships.

Rear Admiral David W. Taylor (1864-1940), Chief
Constructor, US Navy, 1914-1923

The First Division sailed for France-June

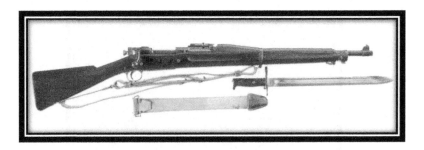

The men were armed with the legendary 1903
Springfield Rifle (and bayonet)

Adm. William S. Sims (1858-1936), Chief of Naval
Forces, Europe, 1917-1919

The War Industries Board-1917

Bernard Baruch (1870-1965), Chairman, War Industries
Board

The official Great War soldier's uniform, based on the British "tunic" model

An officer's uniform was distinguished by banded cuffs

UNIFORM REGULATIONS
UNITED STATES NAVY

NAVY DEPARTMENT
1913
(REVISED TO JANUARY 15, 1917)

Lieutenant
Undress

US Navy uniforms did not change much during the war
from pre-war days

One of the US Navy's most famous, and enduring,
recruitment posters, circa 1917

The infamous "iron ration" from the Great War

"Chow Time"-France-1917

And, once in a while, fresh bread from kitchens just
behind the lines

The 116th Infantry from the 1st Division marches in Paris, July 4th

"Lafayette-We Are Here!"

The First American Soldiers to die in the Great War

Corporal James B. Gresham (1893-1917)

Pvt. Thomas F. Enright
(1887-1917)

Pvt. Merle D. Hay
(1896-1917)

Bayonet Drill-France-1st Division

Getting ready to fight

General Pershing inspects his troops–July...

...as more Doughboys debark at St. Nazaire, ready to join the war effort

The Western Front-1917

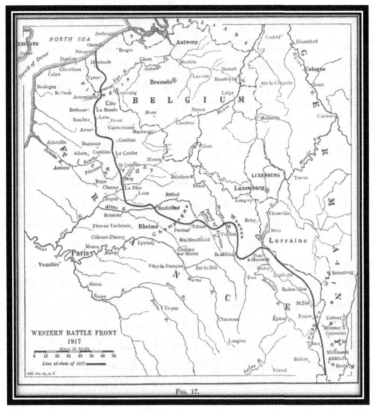

American troops begin to be placed into the line along the "quiet sector," near Lorraine, in August (lower right)

⊙ Americans at War in the Air

As soon as the Great War commenced, some Americans wanted to get into it, even if most of their fellow countrymen and their own government did not. Thousands of American volunteers crossed borders or went overseas to enlist with the Canadians, French, British, Italians, Greeks, Portuguese, Russians and other allied nations—some even went to fight for the Central Powers.

Those Americans who wanted to join the various air services that were springing up would find a warm welcome in Britain and France in particular, especially if they had any experience in aviation whatsoever. Experimental pilots, barnstormers, mail service pilots, flying circus members, and even a few military air service pilots ended up in foreign flight uniforms. Approximately two hundred Americans flew for the Royal Flying Corps (predecessor to the Royal Air Force) and another two hundred and sixty or so (the records are incomplete) joined France's Lafayette Flying Corps (which included the Lafayette Escadrille).

The US Army's own Air Service was slow to get off the ground, literally and figuratively: Recognizing the budding importance of aviation as a combat arm, Congress created, in 1914, an Army Aviation Section to begin to build an "air force." They assigned this nascent Aviation Section to the Signal Corps, which was dominated—no surprise—by communications officers with no training or experience in aviation. Chaos and confusion reigned among competing interests and conflicting priorities. Training of pilots lagged far behind desired outcomes and procurement of aircraft, equipment, parts, and mechanics, was haphazard and uncoordinated. Consequently, when America finally declared war, the Air Section was totally unprepared for effective or sustained combat operations, and would remain so for many months.

Early in 1918, the Air Section was effectively disbanded and an entirely new and separate Air Service was created. Under its own Director and with its new charter, more effective air support for the war began in earnest.

The Army's aviation pioneers faced harrowing conditions: They flew in flimsy, unheated aircraft made of light wood, canvas, and thin wires. Several shot off their own propellers before a synchronizing mechanism was invented that allowed an airplane's machine gun to shoot bullets in between the revolutions of the prop. Pilots had little protection against the numbing cold of altitude and no protection from bullets fired by aerial opponents or shooters on the ground. The planes easily caught fire and many pilots were burned to death before they could land. Early pilots did not carry parachutes. Jumping out of a disabled aircraft was considered "cowardly." It wasn't until after the war that pilots and their commanders finally figured out that trained pilots were actually worth more than the planes themselves.

This is a brief synopsis of the fascinating story of America's involvement with the aviation portion of the Great War:

The Lafayette Escadrille:

All Americans who flew under the banner of France were part of the Lafayette Flying Corps, named, of course, for the Marquis de Lafayette, one of the great heroes of the American War of Independence. As nearly as can be determined, with incomplete records, some one hundred eighty of the approximately two hundred nine pilots trained by the Corps flew in combat. Of these men, sixty-three died, fifty-five in action against the enemy and eight in training accidents. Eleven of the Corps became "aces:" pilots who shot down at least five enemy aircraft. All-in-all, its members destroyed one hundred and ninety-nine enemy planes, and earned numerous Croix de Guerres, Medailles Militaires, and Legions d'Honneur.

A well-known outfit that operated as part of the Lafayette Flying Corps was the similarly named Lafayette Escadrille. This squadron consisted primarily of American pilots operating as one cohesive unit. These aviators were originally dubbed the "Escadrille Americaine;" but, with the United States a neutral country at that time, Germany objected to the name, via diplomatic channels, and it was changed. Many American pilots who fought in the Great War were reported as members of the Lafayette Escadrille when they were not. Only thirty-eight Americans served with the Lafayette Escadrille during its short, two-year history. The other American pilots who were not assigned to the Lafayette Escadrille were scattered throughout the other French fighter, bomber, and observation squadrons. All Americans who flew in French uniforms; however, were veterans of the Lafayette Flying Corps; thus, the confusion.

The unit that became the Lafayette Escadrille was formed in April, 1916, at the urging of two Americans who were serving for France. The first was Dr. Edmund Gros, a San Franciscan by birth, but when the war commenced, one of the directors of the American Hospital in Paris. Dr. Gros was among the first to join up with the French forces and was instrumental in founding the Ambulance Corps for which so many American citizens would volunteer—including Ernest Hemingway. He met up with another American in a French uniform, Norman Prince, in 1915. Prince, a Harvard College and Harvard Law School graduate, was flying as a sergeant-pilot when he conceived the idea to round up some of his American friends and incorporate them into an American flying squadron. Dr. Gros, well known in France for his medical work and his efforts on behalf of the war, used his influence with the French authorities to make Prince's plan a reality.

The new squadron would be very French, right down to its planes, mechanics, uniforms, weapons, and ranks. It would also be commanded by a Frenchman, the very capable and skilled Captain George Thenault. He would be supported by a cadre of five additional French officers.

The makeup of the thirty-eight Americans who dominated the squadron had some interesting characteristics: twenty-eight were already serving or had served in the French forces, seven of those in the Air Service; twenty-three were from the Eastern states including nine from New York; their average age was twenty-six; eleven were the sons of millionaires and thirty of them had attended or graduated from college, including nine from Harvard.

The intrepid pilots of the Lafayette Escadrille initially flew the Nieuport 11, a single seat fighter. Later, in October, 1916, they would transition to the larger Nieuport 17.

The Nieuport 11 was nicknamed Bebe; or "Baby" in French. The aircraft was almost eight feet tall, with a wingspan of nearly twenty-five feet, and a length of nineteen feet. The entire plane weighed less than eight hundred pounds, empty, with a maximum takeoff weight of twelve hundred pounds. It was powered by a nine-cylinder, air cooled, rotary engine that could crank Bebe up to almost one-hundred MPH. The effective range was about two hundred miles and the plane could fly as high as 15,000 feet. Armament consisted of one Lewis or Hotchkiss machine gun mounted above the wing (so that the bullets would not interfere with the propeller).

The Nieuport 17 was slightly longer, taller, and wider. It was a bit heavier and could carry two hundred more pounds. It was slightly faster (110 MPH) and could fly higher (17,400 feet). It's main advantage, however, was its armament: early versions had a better Lewis gun, one that could be re-loaded much more easily, and later models had a synchronized Vickers gun that could shoot in conjunction with the pilot's line-of-sight and through the rotations of the prop.

Both Nieuport models were more advanced than their German competition, which was primarily the Fokker Eindecker ("single wing"). The Nieuports had tighter controls that gave them improved flight characteristics and better maneuverability. It wouldn't take long for the Germans to catch up, however, and even surpass the Nieuports (with improved Fokkers).

The merry and ambitious band of American and French pilots began their active pursuit of the enemy and glory in May of 1916 at the Battle of Verdun. Five days later, the squadron shot down its first enemy aircraft. The pilots of the escadrille would go on to fly over 3,000 sorties before the unit was disbanded and absorbed into the Army Air Service in February, 1918 (as the 103rd Aero Squadron). The daring aviators would lose nine of their own killed in action while racking up forty confirmed and one-hundred probable kills.

The American Squadrons:

In April, 1917, the Army had only 35 qualified pilots with another 51 student pilots in training. The Aviation Section actually had nine times as many planes (280) as designated aviators, but the aircraft were totally unsuited for combat. The planes in inventory consisted mostly of Curtiss Jenny trainers and a few exhausted observation planes left over from the Pancho Villa Expedition. It was clear that drastic measures would have to be taken—and quickly. Fortunately, Congress was in an expansive frame of mind and finally on a war footing. Federal funds became virtually limitless: A bill was passed containing $640 million for aviation, the largest single funding resolution in the history of the US Congress to that time.

Recruitment and training became paramount. An adventurous and energetic reserve officer on the faculty at Yale stepped forward: Major Hiram Bingham III (later a US Senator from Connecticut) organized a consortium of six large universities (later eight) to host aviation ground schools for aspiring recruits. The curriculum was based on the successful Canadian pilot training program. The first new class of 147 student pilots concluded their initial studies in mid-July. By mid-November the enrollment had swollen to 3,140 and, ultimately, before the Armistice, there would be 17,450 successful completions.

At the end of the eight week ground school, aviation cadets (with the unofficial rank and pay of a Private First Class) were advanced to Primary Flight Training. A successful candidate could be designated an aviator and commissioned as a Reserve Second Lieutenant in fifteen to twenty five hours of flight time over a six to eight week course. Unsuccessful candidates remained as privates first class and were made available to the draft. Approximately 15,000 of those who completed ground school made it through primary flight training.

Seventeen hundred of the newly commissioned pilots were sent to France, Britain, or Italy for advanced training on site. Because of aircraft and training backlogs, the French air forces could not absorb all the Americans right away, so over one thousand of these fledglings pilots were given temporary duties as cooks, guards, or general menial laborers until their advancements to full aviator status could be procured.

Back home, another 8,688 of the trained pilots were given advanced training and promoted to First Lieutenant. Most of these pilots were then sent overseas where they were further designated to the burgeoning numbers in pursuit (fighter), bombing, or observation squadrons. Several hundred pilots were kept stateside and turned into flight instructors for those who were immediately behind them.

After a laughable start, the Army Air Service grew rapidly. By the end of the war the 35 initial pilots had turned into more than 17,000 reserve officers, 3,000 regular officers, 10,000 mechanics and another 165,000 enlisted personnel supporting some 7,000 aircraft. These men and planes were scattered among forty flying fields, eight balloon fields, five schools of aeronautics, six air technical schools, and fourteen aircraft depots in the States or at one of nineteen training schools in France, Britain, or Italy.

Because the aircraft production capabilities of the United States were far behind their Allied contemporaries (and would never catch up during the eighteen months of the war) American pilots flew mostly aircraft of French or British manufacture.

To supply the aerial ballet with the machines required, the War Department agreed to purchase, from France, 2,000 SPAD XIII and 1,500 Nieuport 28 pursuit planes as well as 1,500 Breguet-14, B-2 bomber-reconnaissance aircraft. The British supplied a few DeHaviland DH-4B bombers; but, they also provided the design drawings to produce these early two-person bombers to three American companies. The Dayton-Wright Company of Ohio built over 3,100 DH-4B's; General Motors added another 1,500; and, Standard Aircraft Company of

New Jersey added 140. These aircraft were the only American-built planes to serve in the Great War.

The United States also acquired, from France, over 500 Salmson 2, A2, two-seat reconnaissance aircraft and over one-hundred SPAD VII models. The British contributed the S.E.5, a single seat predecessor to the famous Sopwith Camel, which became the primary pursuit training aircraft for American pilots. The S.E. 5 was sturdier, more forgiving, and easier to fly than some of the other models; therefore, it was perfect for training novice aviators.

Nearly forgotten, given all the romantic tales of derring-do contributed by the fixed-wing aviators on the war, was that the United States also fielded a robust observation balloon effort. Thirty-five balloon companies were active in France, with twenty-three of those deployed to the front lines. At one balloon per company, these intrepid observers were charged with detecting enemy troop movements, spotting artillery (both outgoing and incoming), looking for vehicular traffic behind enemy lines, reporting the balloon ascensions of the enemy; and, spying on enemy aircraft many of which became intent on shooting down the very balloons that were observing their movements.

The balloons were the French designed, Goodyear Rubber Company manufactured, Type R craft. They were tethered to the ground at all times and launched and recovered by a hand-operated winch. Filled with hydrogen, they were inherently flammable and especially susceptible to bullets and artillery fire. The air crewmen of each balloon were equipped with parachutes and if the balloon couldn't be recovered in a timely fashion before being fired upon, the balloonists were instructed to jump. Army records collected after the war indicate that balloon pilots and observers were forced to escape from their craft on one-hundred sixteen occasions. Every parachute worked; but, one soldier was killed when burning fragments from the balloon he had just left fell onto his open chute collapsing it before he could safely descend.

Forty-eight American balloons were lost in combat: thirty-five were shot down by enemy planes, twelve were destroyed by ground fire or artillery, and one broke its cable and drifted behind enemy lines where it landed and its two-man crew fell into enemy hands.

For an effort that started out grossly underfunded and totally disorganized, the Army Air Service ended up acquitting itself quite well by Armistice Day. American pilots shot down 781 enemy aircraft and 78 balloons. These are the confirmed numbers: The actual numbers are likely far greater. Many Central Powers aircraft fell behind their own lines and could not be officially witnessed under the rules of that war; therefore, they were not counted in the final tallies.

Air Service losses were 289 airplanes, the 48 balloons mentioned above, 235 airmen killed in action, 130 wounded, 145 captured, and 654 who died of illness or accidents. The men of the Air Service were honored with four Medals of Honor, three-hundred twelve Distinguished Service Crosses, numerous Silver Stars, two-hundred and ten Croix de Guerres from France, twenty-two British Distinguished Flying Crosses and sixty-nine personal decorations from Italy, Portugal, and Romania.

Such were the statistics: And now, in brief, some of the remarkable stories of the individual American airmen who stood behind the numbers and the medals:

William "Billy" Mitchell: Born in Nice, France, while his wealthy parents were on vacation, "Billy" Mitchell (December 29, 1879-February 19, 1936) was, without question, one of the most important founders of the American air power effort. Mitchell, whose father was a wealthy United States Senator from Wisconsin, grew up in Milwaukee and graduated from what is today George Washington University in Washington, DC. Just before graduation in 1899, he enlisted in the 1st Wisconsin Infantry in an effort to get into the Spanish-American War. His father, John, as a sitting US Senator, got "Billy" instant elevation to a 2nd Lieutenant's commission; but, the war ended before young Mitchell saw any action. He elected to stay in the Army, however, and was posted to the

Signal Corps. He served in Cuba, the Philippines; and, in 1901, Alaska, where he distinguished himself by leading an exhaustive effort to open up remote parts of the Territory to telegraph communications. During some of the frozen Alaskan nights, before the Wright Brothers historic flights, Mitchell took time to study early glider experiments, which piqued his interest in the possibilities of manned flight.

Mitchell became a rising star in the Army and by 1906 had been promoted to captain. During the same year he wrote an article in the *Cavalry Journal* confidently stating that future conflicts would very likely be carried out in the air. His opinions were revolutionary and "farfetched" to many in the military, but he proved to be very prescient.

In 1912, he was assigned to the Army General Staff in Washington to represent the Signal Corps. He was the youngest officer, at age 32, to have ever been so posted. He continued, while in that job, to develop his theories on the prospects for military aeronautics. The Signal Corps was, at that time, in charge of Army aviation.

Mitchell was promoted to major in 1916, convinced that whatever career he had ahead of him in the military was in aviation. He was deemed "too old" to attend flight school, however, so he paid out of his own pocket to learn to fly. At the "advanced" age of 38, he was finally given the rating of "junior military aviator." He was also made Deputy Commander of the Signal Corp's Aviation Section.

In April, 1917, Mitchell decided he needed to go to France to study aircraft manufacturing, in which the French were rapidly becoming experts. Within days of his arrival, the United States declared war on Germany. He immediately started meeting with Allied commanders, even before Pershing sailed for France, to discuss employment of air power. When General Pershing finally arrived and set up his headquarters, Mitchell was promoted to lieutenant colonel and assigned to the AEF Staff. He was the first American officer to fly over the German lines, doing so with a French pilot on April 24th.

Mitchell worked tirelessly to get American pilots to France, get them trained, and then into their French or British aircraft. He was aggravated by French pilots having to fly cover over the American lines. With Pershing insisting that American troops fight in their own units, Mitchell likewise believed that it was critical to have American pilots above American troops to maintain effective command and control of ground and air forces.

Colonel Mitchell finally got his first full squadron of Americans into combat in April, 1918, just as the Germans were beginning a major offensive against the Allies. In September, 1918, he led a coordinated attack of nearly 1,500 American, British, French, and Italian aircraft in support of

American ground forces at the battle of St. Mihiel. It was a smashing success: the Allies gained complete air superiority and helped blunt the German ground offensive. Mitchell was promoted to temporary brigadier general and placed in charge of all American air forces in France.

He was not without enemies in his own camp, however. Brash, opinionated, aggressive, and with a flair for attracting the attention of the press, he sometimes pushed too hard. He pressed ahead with building airfields, hangars, and more squadrons. He continued to beat his own drum, sometimes at the expense of his ground-based contemporaries. He was unwittingly sowing the seeds for his own future conflicts with his fellow officers—ending in a famous court martial for "insubordination" in 1925.

There is no question, however, about the importance of "Billy" Mitchell's contributions to the ascendancy of Army air power and its accomplishments in the Great War. His leadership also enabled some of the most famous names in aviation to become successful. Mitchell was awarded both the Distinguished Service Cross and the Distinguished Service Medal for his leadership.

Norman Prince: "Prince" was Norman's surname; but, it could also have been used as a descriptor for this energetic, courageous, adventurous American (August 31, 1887-October 15, 1916). He was born into a very wealthy

American investment banking family who owned an estate called "Princemere," north of Boston. His grandfather had been a Mayor of Boston and had attended Harvard, as did his father. Following in both their footsteps, Norman went to Harvard too, graduating in 1908, followed by Harvard Law School, completing his law degree in 1911. With a passionate interest in aviation, he took flying lessons during law school, but did so using an alias to prevent his father from finding out about it. He knew dad would not approve. Norman was granted his pilot's credential by the Aero Club of America on August 28, 1911, only the 55th person in America to have attained a license.

When France went to war in 1914, it was almost a given that Norman would join up. The family owned an estate in France, too, and Norman spoke French fluently. Sailing to France in January, 1915, he immediately offered his skills to the French Air Service. He was not the only young American to do so, and he soon found himself among a growing number of Americans—many of them also Harvard men—who had also flocked to France. As noted above, the American airmen who volunteered to fly for France were assigned to the Lafayette Flying Corps. This was true for Prince, who was accepted and given the rank of Sergeant Pilot (Americans were not granted French commissions as officers at that time).

It didn't take long, however, for the idea to percolate that the Americans ought to have their own squadron within the Service Aeronautique. Prince, along with Dr. Edmund Gros, Director of the American Hospital in Paris, were the leading advocates for such an "escadrille." Dr. Gros, an American who had the ear of a number of French politicians, helped smooth the process. By April, 1916, the dream became reality, and the "Escadrille Americaine" was founded (German objections, as previously stated, forced a name change soon thereafter to the "Lafayette Escadrille").

Norman Prince was the American most closely associated with the idea of American pilots serving in the war. The Harvard Alumni magazine in its March, 1918, issue gave full credit to him for the establishment of the Lafayette Escadrille and for bringing the aviation side of the war to the attention of the American public.

As a pilot, Prince was credited with participating in 122 combat engagements. His eyesight was poor, and in a later day he most likely would never have qualified for service as a pilot; yet, there he was. Somehow, he managed to down five official kills, making him an "ace," and he was believed to have shot down four other planes, but these could not be confirmed.

Perhaps it was his eyesight, or maybe it was fatigue, oncoming darkness, or all the above; but, in the early evening of October 12, 1916, he crashed. He was returning to his home base after a raid on a German weapons factory when the wheels of his Nieuport caught a telegraph wire near the airfield. His plane flipped over and landed upside down, on top of Prince. He lingered for three days, but his injuries proved fatal. On his deathbed he was finally commissioned and promoted to Sous-Lieutenant and awarded the Legion of Honor. This medal would accompany him to his grave along with a Croix de Guerre and Medaille Militaire.

Prince was initially buried near where he fell, at Luxeuil Air Base, then later re-interred in the Lafayette Escadrille Memorial near Paris. In 1937, though, his father had his body moved to what is now his final resting place, an elaborate marble tomb at the National Cathedral in Washington, DC.

<u>Gervais Raoul Lufbery:</u> He went by "Raoul" but his squadron mates called him "Luff." By early 1918, he was the leading ace of the Lafayette Escadrille and soon to be a Major in the US Army Air Service commanding the new 94th Aero Squadron. Lufbery (March 14, 1885-May 19, 1918) was born in France to an American chemist working in a French chocolate factory and a French mother; who, sadly, died when young Raoul was only a year old. Lufbery's father, Edward, left his young son and two older brothers in the care of maternal grandparents and moved back to America.

At age nineteen, Lufbery decided to "see the world," and left his grandparents' home and wandered for two years, holding down odd jobs in

North Africa, Turkey, the Balkans, and Germany. Finally, in 1906, he decided to visit his father who had, by then, moved to Wallingford, Connecticut, and was trying to eke out a living as a stamp dealer. Ironically, Raoul arrived the day after his father relocated to Europe once again. Undeterred, Lufbery decided to stick it out in Connecticut and spent the next two years living with an older brother and working in a local factory making silver casket handles.

In 1908, Lufbery ventured out again. He journeyed to Cuba, New Orleans, and finally to San Francisco, where he enlisted in the US Army. While in the Army he gained American citizenship, became an expert marksman, and served out the remainder of his enlistment in the Philippines. Then, in 1912, it was onto Japan, China, and India. While in India he met the French aviation pioneer Marc Pourpe who was travelling the world, barnstorming in his Bleriot monoplane. Lufbery and Pourpe struck up a friendship and Pourpe hired Lufbery as his mechanic and advance man. They travelled across Asia and the Middle East, finally ending up in France just as the Great War broke out.

Pourpe immediately volunteered his flying skills to the French air service. Lufbery, as an American, could only enlist in the French Foreign Legion, which he did, but then some strings were somehow pulled, and Lufbery received a transfer to work with

Pourpe, again as his mechanic. Pourpe became a bomber pilot in Escadrille N-23.

The story is murky, much like the day itself; but, somehow either by accident or combat, Pourpe came crashing to his death on December, 2, 1914. Squadron records indicate that the numbing cold aloft caused Pourpe to become "unbalanced" and lose control of his aircraft. Lufbery swore that his friend had been shot down by a German Fokker pilot. Either way, Pourpe was dead and Lufbery was devastated. He swore vengeance and immediately requested transfer to aviation school, which he entered in early 1915.

Lufbery flew bombers initially, but then requested a transfer to fighters: he wanted to shoot down German pilots like the one he believed had killed his friend. Sergeant Lufbery learned to fly the single-seat Nieuports in April, 1916. At this very time, the newly formed Lafayette Escadrille was looking for experienced American pilots. Lufbery, who spoke better French than English, but was nonetheless an American, was scooped up by the Escadrille in May.

Lufbery did not quite fit in, at first, with the mostly East Coast educated, wealthy sons of the elite who comprised the bulk of the pilots of the Lafayette Escadrille. Lufbery was self-made, gruff, unsophisticated and touchy. His Ivy League partners were rollicking, carefree, rowdy, and undisciplined. The novices soon learned to respect and follow the "old man," though. By October Lufbery had become an "ace," something none of the rest of the pilots was even close to achieving. They began to pay attention to his tactics, his dedication to his craft, and his advice.

Lufbery was a perfectionist. He was not afraid to get his hands dirty; and, because of his experiences, he was more often found working with the mechanics than drinking brandy with his elitist buddies. He even cleaned and polished every individual bullet than went into his machine gun canisters, hoping to prevent the gun jams that were common at the time.

Much of his down time was spent with the squadron's two mascots, a couple of lion cubs that had somehow been adopted by the group, probably on one of the frequent drinking sprees in Paris. The lions were named, appropriately, "Whisky" and "Soda." They were particularly attached to Lufbery, who seemed to have some magic bond with them. There are numerous contemporary photos of the lions and Lufbery, used to good public relations advantage by the Escadrille.

By the time America finally entered the war, Lufbery was the most famous of the American pilots and had seventeen kills to his credit. His unofficial tally was probably much higher: he may have shot down as many as fifty or sixty enemy planes, but since most of his scores were behind enemy lines and on solo (unverifiable) combat missions, he was not given the credit he probably deserved. He did not seem to care.

With the United States finally "in it," the American pilots were transferred to US Army squadrons. In November, Lufbery was moved over to the Air Service and placed in command of the newly formed 94th Aero Squadron; and, in January, 1918, promoted to Major. His primary responsibility was training "green" American aviators, something that he found not to his liking, especially since, for several weeks, the new squadron was without the machine guns needed to fly combat missions. Lufbery was good at his job, though, as validated by one of his star pupils: Captain Eddie Rickenbacker, America's top ace (26 kills), told everyone that everything he had learned about combat flying, he had learned from Raoul Lufbery.

On May 19, 1918, with his squadron stationed at Toul, a German reconnaissance plane wandered close to the base. One of Lufbery's students went after the target, but after a series of frustrating attacks, it seemed as if the German was going to elude destruction. Lufbery, watching from the ground, couldn't help himself. His own Nieuport, with all its cleaned and polished bullets, was undergoing maintenance. He took another pilot's plane, the only one standing gassed and ready, and took off in pursuit of the fleeing enemy aircraft.

Lufbery quickly caught up with the lumbering German. He executed one pass, firing. Observers on the ground then saw Lufbery pull up. Apparently, his gun had jammed and he began to work frantically to clear it. The German aircraft turned and fired a burst. One tracer round pierced the unshielded fuel tank and also blew into the cockpit cleanly severing the thumb from Lufbery's right hand, the one on the control stick.

What happened next is not known except the Nieuport caught fire. Lufbery was known to have a fear of being burned to death in the cockpit, but only days before he had clearly stated that if he ever caught on fire, he would not jump: he would attempt to side-slip the plane to a landing, hoping to put out the flames or at least get to the ground safely before being immolated. Lufbery was not wearing a parachute (pilots did not pack them at that time). The Nieuport rolled on its back and Lufbery was either ejected (he wasn't wearing a seat belt) or he jumped, hoping to land in the nearby Moselle River, two hundred feet below. He missed.

Lufbery landed on a spiked garden fence and was killed instantly. By the time his squadron mates reached his lifeless body, he had been taken to the town square and covered in fresh flowers. He was buried near where he fell, and his death was front-page news around the world, especially in France and America. Later, in the 1920's, his remains were moved to the Escadrille Memorial.

Victor Emmanuel Chapman: It is hard to imagine the courage required for an early aviator to take to the skies for aerial combat. The flying machines in use during the Great War were unprotected and filled with flammable materials. Neither gas tanks nor pilots were safe from flying metal and incendiary bullets. The survivability of pilots in the Great War was often measured in weeks, not months, and certainly not years. Some brave American flyer would be the first to die, and that sad distinction fell to young Victor Chapman (April 17, 1890-June 24, 1916).

Chapman was born in New York, but after the death of his mother in 1898 he and his father moved to France where Victor obtained dual citizenship. He returned to the United States to attend Harvard and graduated in 1913. He relocated back to Paris to take up the study of architecture but when the war commenced, he decided to join up. As a Private in the French Foreign Legion, he saw action in the trenches along the Somme. After being slightly wounded he decided to fall in with some of his Harvard friends who were volunteering for aviation.

He successfully found his way into the Lafayette Escadrille, completed training as a pursuit pilot, and was promoted to Sergeant Pilot. On June 17, 1916, Chapman was flying a mission near Verdun when he was pounced on by four German fighters. Only with skill and luck was he able to extract himself from a death-defying situation. He did receive a nasty scalp wound, however, when a German machine gun bullet grazed his skull during the harrowing encounter. One week later, on June 24th, he was taking a basket of oranges to a wounded compatriot when he stumbled onto a dogfight between four German fighters and two Americans, including Norman Prince. He decided to assist, and as he maneuvered into position two German planes, one in front and one in back, boxed him in. The trailing German fired a burst into Chapman's plane and several rounds struck Chapman, killing him instantly. His Nieuport continued ahead until it nosed into the ground, near the town of Duaumont, at full speed.

After Chapman's death a very poignant volume of his war writings to his father was published in his name. "Letters From France." became a contemporary classic. Chapman was buried at the Meuse-Argonne American Cemetery and rests there still.

Kiffin Yates Rockwell: The first aerial victory of the war by an American was scored on May 18, 1916, when 24-year old Kiffin Rockwell (September 20, 1892-September 23, 1916), flying solo in a balky, troubled Nieuport, managed to gun down a two-man German observation plane over the Alsace battlefield.

Rockwell may have earned another first in the Great War: some records indicate that he was possibly the first American to see combat; but, the proof is not totally conclusive. If not *the* first, he was certainly one of the first. He ended up in the uniform of a French Foreign Legionnaire in early August, 1914. In May of 1915, while fighting in the trenches manning a machine gun, Rockwell was shot through the right leg. He ended up convalescing in a Paris hospital for six weeks. Rather than return to the trenches, he looked up at the skies and requested a transfer to the newly formed Lafayette Escadrille. He was among the first group of Americans selected.

Originally from Newport, Tennessee, Rockwell had kicked around in his youth, first attending VMI, then the US Naval Academy (briefly) before joining an older brother at Washington and Lee University in Virginia. In 1912, Rockwell left college (before graduating) and travelled westward. At age nineteen, he opened an advertising agency in San Francisco, and then, in 1913, moved to Atlanta and joined an agency there.

As soon as the war broke out, Rockwell and his brother determined they were going to volunteer, and off they sailed to France. His brother, Paul, was also in the French Foreign Legion and also wounded, but more seriously than Kiffin. Paul was determined medically unfit for further service and, instead, settled in Paris as a war correspondent for the *Chicago Daily News*. When Kiffin was posted to the Lafayette Escadrille, brother Paul followed Kiffin's progress, as well as that of the other

Americans, and became the unofficial publicist for the squadron.

Imagine Paul's joy when his little brother became the first American to score in aerial combat—and be awarded both the Croix de Guerre and the Medaille Militaire. Imagine, too, his immense sadness when Kiffin was soon thereafter (September 23rd) engaged in a duel with a two-man German reconnaissance plane and drilled through the heart. He crashed among French trenches much like the ones he and his brother had manned so valiantly. Kiffin Rockwell was the second American aviator, after Victor Chapman, to die in the Great War.

<u>Edward Vernon "Eddie" Rickenbacker</u>: From stories of lives cut short, we come to one lived to the fullest. "Eddie," or sometimes "Fast Eddie" Rickenbacker seemed to have lived several lives in one. He certainly had more than his fair share of brushes with death, too, but somehow managed to survive to the ripe old age of 82. Born in Columbus, Ohio; October 8, 1890, he died of a stroke while on a trip to Zurich, Switzerland; July 23, 1973.

Rickenbacker, who had amassed considerable fame as a race car driver prior to the war, didn't get into uniform until after America declared war. Even then, because he had quit school after seventh grade, he was not considered "educated enough" for pilot training. Instead, Sergeant First

Class Rickenbacker arrived in France in late June, 1917, to serve in aircraft maintenance at the American flight training base at Issoudon. Because of his skill, he was soon commissioned but for duty as an engineer, not as a pilot. He would compensate by sneaking in flight lessons during his off duty time.

He was soon an accomplished pilot but his superiors didn't want to lose him as an engineer. Only when he secured an adequate replacement was he given his junior pilot's wings and assigned to the 94th Aero Squadron. He would make up for lost time at astonishing speed.

In the space of less than thirty days, we has an ace, having five confirmed kills. An ear infection grounded him for several weeks, but in September he came roaring back again shooting down two of Germany's newest fighters, a couple of Fokker D. VII's, on the 14th. Ten days later he was promoted to Captain and made commanding officer of the squadron.

By Armistice Day, Rickenbacker had 26 confirmed kills to his credit (21 aircraft of various types plus 5 balloons) and became the "top ace" of the Americans in the war. His list of honors included a remarkable nine Distinguished Service Crosses and two Croix de Guerres. Later, in 1930, he was belatedly awarded the Medal of Honor by President Herbert Hoover. He elected to leave the Army in 1919, and was granted the rank of Major.

He felt he had not earned the advancement, however, and continued to refer to himself, for the rest of his long life, as "Captain Rickenbacker."

The Captain went on to marry, in 1922, Miss Adelaide Durant, a union that lasted for fifty-one years, right up until his death. He founded an auto company, owned the Indianapolis Motor Speedway for a time, and co-founded Eastern Airlines, which he ran as CEO until 1959. He survived a major airline crash, a WW II ditching that set him adrift in the South Pacific for 24 days, and late in life became a prized motivational speaker, especially on issues related to his well known conservatism and the Cold War.

"Eddie" Rickenbacker was, without question, the greatest and best known American aviation figure to come out of the Great War, and one of only four United States airmen to be awarded the Medal of Honor for his service in that war.

Quentin Roosevelt: There are many dimensions to the tragic story of Quentin Roosevelt, youngest son of former President Theodore Roosevelt. Those who knew the Roosevelts directly are often quoted as saying that of their children, Quentin was the one most like his father, intellectually, emotionally, and adventurously. He had all the fire and spunk of his "old man" and it was clear that he was his father's favorite.

When the Great War started, the old "Bull Moose" himself petitioned his friend General

Pershing for command of a division, which he pledged to raise himself, and then include all four of his sons in the ranks. Pershing endorsed the idea, but President Wilson did not. Theodore would spend the war raising money and giving speeches instead. All four of his sons would serve, though, and each one gallantly. Even the President's youngest daughter, Ethel, would see duty as a nurse in France. Ted, Jr., led a battalion of infantry. Kermit was a British officer in a machine gun corps in Iraq before accepting a US Army artillery commission. Archie was also an Army infantry officer. Quentin chose the Air Service.

To get to France and into flying, Quentin (November 19, 1897-July 14, 1918) had to drop out of Harvard after his sophomore year in 1917. He joined the 1st Reserve Aero Squadron, which conducted training at Mineola Airfield on Long Island. That field is still in use today, and was later renamed Roosevelt Field in Quentin's honor.

On July 23, 1917, Quentin said goodbye to his fiancé, Flora Payne Whitney, granddaughter of the fabulously wealthy Cornelius Vanderbilt, at Pier 23 in New York and sailed for France. Over the next year he served as a supply officer at the large American base at Issoudon, and trained as a pursuit pilot. The flying did not come easily to him, but in true Roosevelt fashion he stuck with it, never giving up.

He finally received his pilot's wings in December and transferred out of supply and into full time status as an aviator. In recognition of his hard earned skill, he was not immediately posted to a front line combat unit, but held back to instruct new pilots: The powers-that-be seemed to appreciate his great good humor and ability to turn adversity into advantage—something that many of the young men moving into aviation, with all of its challenges and hazards, needed to grasp.

At the end of June, twenty year old Quentin got his orders, at last, to a front line unit, the 95th Aero Squadron, "the "Kicking Mules." On the day he left for the front, a large group of his students cheered him on, promising to come rescue him if he ever got shot down behind enemy lines. Quentin wrote about that to Flora, saying, "So I left with a big lump on my throat, for it's nice to know that your men have liked you."

Roosevelt's first day of actual aerial combat, July 5th, was not an auspicious one for him, but what he penned about those hours, in a letter home, was quite powerful in terms of describing the emotions he was experiencing.

During the morning, Roosevelt and several of his squadron mates were out on a patrol. The Nieuport 28 he was flying was giving him fits (he did not particularly like the Nieuports, except for conducting acrobatics). The engine had been cutting in and out; but, typical Roosevelt, he almost willed the plane to work and pressed ahead, not wanting to fall behind the others. The patrol was surprised and overtaken from behind by a single German Fokker who broke off from a larger formation. Sure enough, right at that moment, Roosevelt's engine stopped cold. He later wrote: *"I'm free to confess I was scared blue...I was behind the formation and he had all the altitude. So I pushed on the stick, prayed for motor, and watched out of the corner of my eye to see his elevators go down, and have his tracers shooting by me. However, for some reason, he didn't attack, instead he took a few general shots at the lot and then swung back to his formation."* Roosevelt's engine coughed to life again, and he made it back to base.

He went up again that same afternoon, but in a different aircraft. The patrol found another group of German fighters. This time, his gun jammed and he was helpless to contribute anything to the aerial dueling. The patrol lost two of their own, but managed to shoot down one of the enemy. Of this engagement he wrote: *"I was doubtful before, for I thought I might get cold feet or something, but you don't... You get so excited that you forget everything except getting the other fellow, and trying to dodge the tracers when they start streaking past you."*

Genuinely liked by the other pilots, and without a single ounce of the pretentiousness that he might have commanded as a privileged son of an ex-President, Quentin Roosevelt settled in and became a regular, just "one of the fellows." He was known, however, for his aggressiveness, his boldness, and his determination to succeed. He took great risks—unnecessary risks, some said. In these attributes he was exactly like his father, who expected his sons to come home alive covered in glory, or righteously dead on their shields, at least metaphorically.

On July 10th, Roosevelt took the first step toward what he hoped would be his triumphant service in the war: he shot down his first enemy plane. The excitement he put into his description of the event leaps off the page; yet, the words and phrases he used might very well detail the results of a tennis match, and not the life-and-death struggle it truly was :

"I was out on high patrol with the rest of my squadron when we got broken up due to a mistake in the formation. I dropped into a turn of a vrille (twisting, like the tendril of a vine)—these planes have so little surface that at five thousand you can't do much with them. When I got straightened out I couldn't spot my crowd anywhere, so...I decided to fool around a little before going home, as I was just over the lines. I turned and circled for five minutes or so, and then suddenly...I saw three planes in formation. At first I thought they were Boche (German), but as they paid little attention to me I finally decided to chase them, thinking they were part of my crowd, so I started after them at

full speed. I thought at the time it was a little strange...that they should be going almost straight into Germany, but I had plenty of gas so I kept on.

"They had been going absolutely straight and I was nearly in formation when the leader did a turn, and I saw to my horror that they had white tails with black crosses on them. Still I was so nearby them that I thought I might pull up a little and take a crack at them. I had altitude on them, and what was more they hadn't seen me, so I pulled up, put my sights on the end man, and let go. I saw my tracers going all around him, but for some reason he never even turned, until all of a sudden his tail came up and he went down in a vrille. I wanted to follow him but the other two had started around after me, so I had to cut and run."

Four days later, July 14th, was Bastille Day in France. It was raining in Paris, a few miles to the northwest, but the Allies were nonetheless staging a large parade along the Champs-Elysees in honor of the great national holiday. The Germans, on the other hand, had a different sort of celebration in mind: A major offensive was scheduled to kick off the following morning in the Chateau-Thierry vicinity. The German squadrons in the area had strict orders to stay aloft at all times and prevent any Allied observation of the great marshalling and preparation efforts being undertaken behind the German lines.

Naturally, rather than stifle interest, the significant amount of traffic in the air around the German staging area stimulated the curiosity of the Allies and they launched numerous patrols, including one from the 95th Aero Squadron. The early morning mission was led by Lieutenant Edward Buford (1891-1962) and consisted of four Nieuport pursuit planes and a two-seat Sopwith observation plane from the 88th Aero Squadron. The Sopwith would take photos of the activity behind the German lines, with protection from Buford's group.

No sooner had the photo mission been completed, and the Americans headed for home, than they were "jumped" by a seven-plane detachment of German Fokkers. Outnumbered almost two-to-one, and facing high winds, clouds, and blowing fog, Buford decided discretion was the better part of valor and ordered his men to get back across the lines. Besides, the photos were the first priority, and the observation plane needed to get back safely.

In the general confusion, the formation was scattered. One Nieuport broke away to tackle a group of three Fokkers. Roosevelt's eagerness had overcome his judgment. Buford wrote, shortly after the day's events, *"I tried to keep an eye on all of our fellows but we were hopelessly separated and out-numbered nearly two to one. About a half a mile away I saw one of our planes with three Boche on him, and he seemed to be having a pretty hard time with them, so I shook the two I was maneuvering with and tried to get over to him, but before I could reach them, [his] machine turned over on its back and plunged down out of control. I realized it was too late to be of any assistance...."*

In the melee, machine gun bullets from three different Fokkers raked over Roosevelt's plane. Two bullets struck him squarely in the head and killed him instantly. The Nieuport, damaged and out of control, spiraled into the earth below. All three German pilots took credit for downing Roosevelt, especially after they discovered later who it was; but, the pilot who most probably fired the fatal shots was Sergeant-Pilot Carl-Emil Graper of Jasta (Fighter Squadron) 50. If so, it was Graper's first and only "kill" of the war.

Roosevelt's plane fell behind the German lines. His body was removed from the mangled wreck and laid on the ground beside his aircraft. A nearby German photographer took a photo of the gruesome scene. When the corpse was searched for identity papers, a German officer discovered a love letter from Flora in Quentin's pocket. It was then the astonished German's discovered they had killed Teddy Roosevelt's son. With great respect, flowers, and parts of his crashed airplane, the Germans buried Quentin where he fell, and immediately contacted the Foreign Office, who respectfully cabled the State Department.

President Roosevelt received quiet notice of his son's death in advance of the story breaking worldwide. It was said that he went to the barn on his Sagamore Hill Estate, in Oyster Bay, Long Island, and buried his face in the mane of Quentin's favorite horse, and wept for hours. The elder Roosevelt, knowing full well he had sent his sons to war, was shattered. He never recovered and within six months, he, too, would be dead.

The death photo of Quentin lying beside his plane was—distastefully—made into a propaganda postcard. A few circulated before an outraged State Department objected and the German Foreign Office quietly had the offending cards withdrawn and destroyed.

Soon after Quentin's death, his grave fell within the shifting lines of the Allies. It became a shrine, but not a permanent one: In 1955, at the request of the Roosevelt family, Quentin's body was moved so he could lie alongside his eldest brother, Theodore Roosevelt, Jr., at the American Cemetery at Normandy. Ted, Jr. had courageously led his troops ashore at Omaha Beach on D-Day but died a month later, of a heart attack.

Frank Luke, Jr.: The story of the remarkable Frank Luke, Jr., (May 19, 1897-September 29, 1918) flashes across the skies over France almost as if it were a meteor. He was the second highest scoring American aviator of the war (behind "Eddie" Rickenbacker) but achieved all eighteen of his verified kills during an eight day, ten sortie rampage in September, 1918, just two months after he had finished his training, in France.

Born in Arizona to (ironically) German parents who had emigrated to America in 1873, Luke was a rambunctious boy who grew up in a large family among the copper mines of the arid, dusty southwest. As a teenager, he earned extra money by engaging in bare-knuckle boxing matches. When America finally entered the war, he immediately enlisted in the Signal Corps. He requested and was accepted for pilot training, which he breezed through at training bases in Texas and California. He was commissioned a 2nd Lieutenant, received his Junior Aviator wings and was shipped off to Europe for final training.

When he arrived in France in March, 1918, he completed the last phases of his instruction and was assigned to the 27th Aero Squadron in July. Flying a mix of Sopwith Camels, Nieuports, and SPADs, the 27th was a fighter, close air support, and "balloon busting" squadron. Luke, in fact, was nicknamed the "Arizona Balloon Buster" in that fourteen of his eighteen scores were German balloons. These stationary targets were not as easy to down as one might think: because the balloons were both critical and defenseless, they were often surrounded by artillery installations and machine guns, making them very lethal objectives for the flimsy and slow-moving aircraft of the era. Nonetheless, Frank Luke became particularly expert at blowing them out of the sky. Luke worked with a partner pilot who tried to suppress ground fire by strafing while Luke shot up the balloons themselves: it was a tactic that worked quite well—until it didn't.

There are conflicting stories on how Luke met his fate. His partner (2nd Lieutenant Joe Wehner) had been shot down and killed by a German pilot on September 18th, the same day Luke shot down two balloons and two enemy planes. After this, Luke flew alone. On September 29th, he took off on a mission behind the German lines to tackle three balloons that had been spotted aloft. He downed each one of them, under murderous fire. After his last pass, he dipped below a nearby hill for cover, seeking an escape route back across the lines. Unbeknownst to Luke, there was a German machine gun nest on the crest of the hill. The gunners, who at that moment were actually above Luke, fired down on him. One bullet struck Luke near the right shoulder, passed entirely through his body, and exited his left side. The wound was not immediately fatal, but it was mortal.

Luke managed to land his plane in an open field after strafing a German position nearby. His intention, apparently, was to get to the safety of some brush on the edge of a nearby stream and await rescue. He staggered from his plane, and made it about two hundred yards before surviving German soldiers caught up with him. He un-holstered his pistol and fired all its rounds at the

Germans, hitting no one. The Germans did not fire back, because at that moment, Luke fell over dead. The Germans retrieved his body and buried him, respectfully, in the cemetery of the nearby village of Murvaux. He was later re-interred at the American Meuse-Argonne Memorial Cemetery.

Luke's flash-in-the-pan but astonishing war record would lead to him becoming the first American aviator of the Great War to be granted the Medal of Honor (1919).

Eugene James ("Jacques") Bullard: If Eugene Bullard's life story wasn't ripped from the pages of a novel, it should have been: perhaps a collaboration between Victor Hugo and Mark Twain. Born into a large family from Columbus, Georgia, his father was African-American and his mother a Creek Indian. His father's family arrived in America, as slaves, at the time of the American Revolution. The family that had once owned them was French and had fled Haiti during that nation's slave rebellions. Both French and English were spoken in the Bullard home. Eugene's mother died when he was just five, leaving his father to raise seven children.

When Eugene (October 9, 1895-October 12, 1961) was only eight, his father was nearly lynched by a group of white supremacists who were still fuming over the outcome of the Civil War. His father had often told him about their French heritage, and that, unlike America, France was a

251

country where anyone would be welcome to live and find work, regardless of the color of their skin. To an impressionable young boy, this sounded much better than continually facing the hatred of bigoted Southern whites.

Equipped with only with a second grade education and the clothes on his back, he decided, at age eleven, to leave home and somehow find his way to France. He would eventually make it, but it would take him several years. For the first year, he lived with Gypsies, who taught him to work with horses. He became a jockey and actually won a few races, squirreling away money to escape to Europe. He made his way to Norfolk, Virginia, where—then age twelve—he stowed away aboard a German freighter headed for Aberdeen, Scotland.

From Aberdeen, he made his way to Glasgow, then Liverpool, England. Along the way he held odd jobs as a longshoreman, a helper on a fish wagon, and dodging balls for coins at an amusement park. Any spare time he had, he spent at a local gym, lifting weights, trying to add mass to his skinny frame.

He started helping out around the gym, particularly with the boxers. He had a winning way about him, and was soon allowed to step into the ring himself, as a sparring partner. He proved better than that, however, and quickly found himself on the boxing card as a lightweight. He had just turned sixteen.

Asked to join a touring group of boxers, he went all about Europe; first to Russia, then to Germany; and, finally to Paris. Eugene stepped into a ring at the Elysee Montmartre on November 28, 1913, and from that moment forward, he knew he belonged, as he had hoped, in France. He left the travelling troop and settled in Paris, welcomed into the local boxing scene.

When war broke out the next summer, Eugene was ready to step up and fight for his adopted country. He was, however, too young—in France the enlistment age was nineteen, and even at that, as an American, he could only join the French Foreign Legion. On October 9, his nineteenth birthday, he did just that.

For the next two years, as a member of the Moroccan Division of the Legion, Eugene Bullard saw some of the toughest trench fighting of the war. Casualties were horrific. Bullard was in many battles where he fought hand-to-hand, once with just a bayonet. On September 25th, 1915, during the Battle of Champagne, Bullard's Legionnaire outfit started the day with 500 men. By that evening, only thirty-one answered roll call—a 94% casualty rate. Bullard survived with only a slight head wound, but his company, which hardly existed any longer, was disbanded and the few survivors were sent to the legendary 170th French Infantry, a front line outfit nicknamed the "Swallows of Death." Bullard was quickly named the "Black Swallow of Death."

In February of 1916, the 170th entered the maelstrom that would become the ten-month Battle of Verdun. A quarter million men would die, another one hundred thousand would end up missing, and another three hundred thousand wounded—Eugene Bullard among them. He was so badly shot up, the doctors thought he might never walk again. He was sent to a hospital in Lyons and also awarded the Croix de Guerre and the Medaille Militaire for his courage.

Ironically, since he was no longer fit for duty in the Infantry, the only combat arm open to him was the French Flying Corps. A friend bet Bullard $2,000 he could not pass the pilot's tests and get his wings. Bullard promptly hauled himself out of his convalescent bed and proved his friend wrong. On May 5, 1917, Bullard completed French pilot's school, got his wings, collected $2,000, and became the first African-American fighter pilot in history.

Bullard had been in the war for three years, earned over a dozen decorations for valor, had been wounded four times, but was still just a corporal. Almost all of the white French pilots, including a number of Americans, were at least Sergeant-Pilots, and many were lieutenants and captains. Bullard, after getting his wings, was only rated "sergeant"—the highest rank he would attain while he was in active service.

After the United States joined the action, all American pilots were summoned to the Army Air Service (not all chose to accept). Bullard wanted to join them. He was, by this time, an experienced combat pilot with at least two probable kills to his credit. He took and passed the physical, but "somehow" his application for transfer was ignored for the remainder of the war.

He continued to fly with his old French unit until November, 1917, when, after a 24-hour pass in Paris, he got into a scuffle with a stiff-necked French lieutenant over—of all things—a seat on a truck returning to base. The French lieutenant kicked Bullard in the chest to push him off the truck. Bullard grabbed the man's boot and tossed him into a muddy ditch. It was, in reality, much ado about nothing; yet, an enlisted soldier striking an officer was a serious offense. Because of Bullard's impressive collection of decorations and long service, he was not court martialed. He was, however, removed from flight status and sent back to his old infantry unit, the 170th , where he spent the balance of the war performing menial tasks.

Bullard was discharged from the French Army in October, 1919. He was a national hero and somewhat of a celebrity in Paris. He turned that celebrity into ownership of a nightclub and marriage to a wealthy French girl, with whom he had two daughters and a son (who died in infancy).

As the Nazis filtered into Paris in the late 1930s, Gene agreed to use his club to spy on the German patrons who flocked to his bar and his jazz shows. It was a dangerous game and once, in 1939, he was almost killed for his efforts.

When WW II came along, and by that time single once more, Eugene left Paris to find his old unit. He left his two daughters with the Resistance. In Orleans, he fell in with some French troops who were battling the Nazis. The group came under heavy attack and was nearly wiped out. Bullard was severely injured, yet again. Friends with the French forces managed to get Bullard bandaged up, and smuggled him into Spain with help from an American Consul in Biarritz. From Spain, he made his way to Portugal, then New York City where he lived out the remainder of his days in Spanish Harlem. His last job was as an elevator operator at Rockefeller Center.

His fame was largely unknown in the United States, but not in France. He was named a Knight of the Legion of Honor in 1959, and hugged in public in New York City by Charles de Gaulle in 1960, embraced as a true French hero.

He died in 1961, of complications from stomach cancer, and was laid to rest with full honors in the French War Officers Federation Cemetery, in Flushing, New York.

Realizing too late what they had missed, the United States Air Force finally recognized the first

African-American fighter pilot in history in 1994 when they posthumously commissioned the old warrior a 2nd Lieutenant in the USAF.

Ernest R. Bleckley & Harold E. Goettler: These two intrepid aviators were half of the four airmen (plus Frank Luke and "Eddie" Rickenbacker) to receive Medals of Honor for aerial heroics in the Great War. They are chronicled together because they earned their medals together, on the same mission, and died together achieving their glory. It is truly a story that is, as they say, "the stuff of legends." First, a little background on both aviators:

Harold Ernest Goettler's parents were natives of Germany who had emigrated to Chicago, where Harold was born in 1890. Harold grew into an impressive young man, tall for his era at 6'3" and weighed a strapping 220 pounds with blond hair and blue eyes. Favoring his parents adopted city, he enrolled at the University of Chicago where he became a star athlete in both basketball and football. He was also an excellent student and graduated, in 1914, with honors. Within weeks of his graduation, Germany declared war on France and Great Britain. Since his birth country had declared neutrality, Harold unhesitatingly went to the German Consulate in Chicago seeking permission, and papers, to travel to Germany where he intended to enlist and fight for his parent's native land. The Consul talked him out of it declaring that the war was going to be very short and he would never get processed in time to see any action. Believing what he was told, Harold set aside his quest and went into the real estate business.

Very soon, events began to occur that would change his feelings: The Lusitania was cruelly dispatched; the Zimmerman telegram showed a duplicitous side to German foreign policy; and, unrestricted u-boat warfare was taking a toll on American shipping and innocent citizens. Harold's loyalties switched to favor his native land and he enlisted in the US Army Signal Reserve Corps in July, 1917, as a Private First Class. He was called up for duty in August at the Military Aeronautics School of the University of Illinois, where he volunteered for pilot training. From October until January 1918, he trained at Camp Mohawk flight school in Canada and Taliaferro Field in Texas. He received his commission as a 2nd Lieutenant in February and was assigned to the 28th Aero Squadron in England for final flight training. He completed his training in August and was awarded his Junior Pilot's Wings and sent to the 50th Aero Squadron, an observation squadron flying the only American-made planes to see service in the war, the redoubtable DeHaviland DH-4's.

In June of 1917, Kansas native Erwin R. Bleckley was living the genteel, rural, middle class life of a twenty-two year old bank teller at the 4th National Bank of Wichita. When his country called, however, he rallied to the colors. He wanted very much to join the Air Service; but, his parents objected, claiming it was just too dangerous. Bowing to their desires, he enlisted in the Kansas National Guard as a Private in the Field Artillery. A month later, a spot for a 2nd Lieutenant became available, and he was selected. A month after that, his unit was called up and reorganized s the 130th Field Artillery.

After further training, the unit was shipped to France and arrived in March, 1918. As luck would have it, Bleckley, far away from home, was going to get his chance to join the Air Service after all: a call went out for artillery officers to serve as airborne forward artillery observers. Bleckley stepped forward immediately. He went to the Observer's School at Tours, graduated, received the distinctive Observer's Badge, and was assigned to the 50th Aero Squadron on August 14th.

Goettler, promoted to 1st Lieutenant, and Bleckley were paired up as a team almost immediately after each arrived at the 50th. Their squadron was known as the "Dutch Girl Squadron." The men had adopted the well-known "Little Dutch Girl" logo from a popular cleanser, which meant, to them, that they were going to "clean up on Germany." The logo was painted on the sides of all eighteen DH-4 "Liberty" planes in the squadron and all the men wore matching pins above the right breast pockets of their uniforms.

259

The team of Bleckley and Goettler flew their first combat mission on September 12th: It was the first day of the St. Mihiel Offensive and the pair flew in support of the advance of the 90th Infantry Division, scouting ahead of the troops as they pushed forward. They flew similar missions over each of the next five days, and Bleckley's spotting proved so successful that he was recommended for promotion to 1st Lieutenant.

Toward the end of September, on the 26th, the 50th Aero began supporting the Meuse-Argonne Offensive from a new aerodrome in Remicourt. The 77th Infantry Division got the assignment to spearhead the attacks into the densely wooded forests. Hardly anything went as planned. French units were supposed to be supporting the left flank and another American division, the 92nd, the right. The French units were stalled and couldn't advance under the heavy German opposition. The Americans on the right proceeded much more slowly and cautiously. The net result was that over 500 men from the 307th and 308th Infantry Regiments, and one company from the 306th Machine Gun Battalion, pushed further ahead than anyone. When the entire advance was called off, these men did not get the message to pull back, and as a result became completely encircled by the Germans. In hours, they became known to history as "The Lost Battalion," and for the next six days would have to fight off one German assault after another as they desperately battled for their lives.

Rescue efforts got under way immediately, once the battalion's predicament became known, but the problem was that no one knew exactly where the trapped men were. Observation flights were attempted, but the forest was so thick, the ground could not be seen. The 50th began flying missions looking for the Lost Battalion on October 2nd, but they were searching in all the wrong places.

The Lost Battalion ran out of food, ran low on ammunition, and could only get water by crawling under heavy fire to a nearby stream. Every messenger the commander, Major Charles Whittlesey, sent was killed or captured. The few carrier pigeons the battalion had with them became the only means of communication. Whittlesey requested artillery support by carrier pigeon but the wrong coordinates were somehow entered. Soon thereafter, artillery shells began raining down on the unlucky Americans. The last carrier pigeon was sent with a desperate plea: "For heaven's sake stop it (the artillery)."

On October 5th, the commander of the 77th Division asked for additional help from the 50th Aero to locate his trapped men and re-supply them from the air. The squadron flew four missions that day until bad weather forced a halt to the search. On the morning of October 6th, the 50th flew another thirteen missions. Air crews attempted to drop food, medical supplies and even more carrier pigeons. One drop was right on top of a cloth panel that had been laid out as a target; but, it turned out that the Germans had placed it there as a ruse. It worked: the Germans received all the supplies, the Americans got none. Worse, the 50th Aero had three aircraft completely shot up, and several aviators were seriously wounded.

The first mission of the afternoon was flown by Goettler and Bleckley. They, too, dropped supplies on what they thought might be the position of the trapped Americans, but it was not. Their DH-4, Aircraft #2, was shot full of holes. They barely made it back, and their plane was deemed unflyable. It didn't stop the determined aviators, though. They borrowed Aircraft #6 from a pilot who had been wounded and could no longer fly. Their squadron commander actually tried to dissuade the two from attempting another mission saying the task was becoming exceedingly hazardous. Bleckley shouted back, "Well make the delivery or die in the attempt!"

Goettler still did not know exactly where the Lost Battalion was located, but he reasoned that he could certainly locate the Germans: they would be the ones shooting at them. Using his big, lumbering DH-4 as a target, he side slipped and jockeyed the plane over the target area. Bleckley, in the rear seat, plotted where the machine gun and rifle bullets were coming from. Those would be the German positions: the area where they weren't receiving fire must, by process of elimination, be where the Americans were located. Bleckley plotted that site, and it was, as it turned out, exactly correct.

As DH-4 Number 6 pulled up and out of a ravine, headed back with the proper coordinates, Lt. Goettler was struck in the head by a machine gun bullet and killed instantly. Bleckley, in the back seat, could do nothing to control the aircraft, which floated out over the French lines then spun lazily into the ground. Bleckley was thrown from the aircraft and landed in a heap with internal injuries that would prove mortal. As Bleckley was being transported to a nearby field hospital, he died, but the French soldiers discovered, in his cockpit, the map with the proper coordinates for the Lost Battalion. The map was rushed to the American lines and handed up to the headquarters of the 77th Division. The besieged men were finally pinpointed. A relief battalion was organized immediately and sent to the scene. They finally broke through and rescued the survivors early in the morning of October 8th. Of the original 554 men in the Lost Battalion, 194 walked out of the forest alive.

The courageous sacrifices of Goettler and Bleckley were immediately recognized by a posthumous award to each airman's family of the Distinguished Service Cross; but, the Army Decorations Board decided to upgrade the awards to both men to the Medal of Honor in 1922. It was fitting recognition for a story of indomitable courage and sacrifice.

David Sinton Ingalls (January 28, 1899-April 26, 1985): The recitation of interesting personalities in American aviation during the Great War would not be complete if it did not mention the US Navy's first ever "ace"—and the Navy's only ace of the Great War. David S. Ingalls was born into "American royalty," connected on his mother's side, to the powerful Taft family of Ohio, and on his father's side to prominent railroad men and industrialists. Later, he would marry the granddaughter of the founder of Standard Oil. Ingalls was educated at St. Paul's School and matriculated at Yale in 1916 where he signed on with the First Yale Unit, which quickly turned into the Naval Reserve Flying Corps. He had his pilot's license soon thereafter and became Naval Aviator Number 85 in March, 1917. Called to active duty in April, he was sent to further training in Palm Beach, then Huntington, Long Island, and finally off to Europe in December. More training ensued in France and England. Because the US Navy did not maintain operating land bases of its own in Europe during the war, Ingalls, promoted to Lieutenant, Junior Grade, was assigned to 213 Squadron of the Royal Air Force in July, 1918.

In August, he began flying in combat and quickly scored a victory. Flying a Sopwith Camel, he shot down a German observation plane on the 11th and another on the 21st. In September, he downed a Rumpler reconnaissance plane, a German balloon, and a Fokker fighter, his fifth "kill," which qualified him as an "ace," the first in US Navy history.

After the war, Ingalls would return to Yale and graduate, then move on to Harvard Law School where he obtained his law degree in 1923. Over a long life of achievement, Ingalls would dabble in politics, serve as Assistant Secretary of the Navy, don his Navy uniform once again in WW II, commanding the Pearl Harbor Naval Air Station and rising to the rank of Rear Admiral in the Naval Reserve.

The US Navy air effort during the Great War started off with less than fifty pilots, fewer than 240 enlisted men, and 54 aircraft and one operational base at Pensacola, Florida. At the end of the war, there were over 2,500 pilots in Europe alone, supported by 22,000 enlisted men, and 400 planes. Bases had been established in France, the Azores, the Panama Canal Zone and even Canada. At home, there were an additional 4,000 officers, 10,000 more enlisted men , and twelve operational bases under construction to support another 1,600 aircraft, 12 airships, and 215 balloons. It was a remarkable expansion in a very short period of time.

This has been a summary look at some of the most interesting men to populate the aviation effort conducted by Americans in the Great War. There were, of course, many others who served, fought, died, or survived. All of them, in some way, contributed to building up the importance of aviation as a combat arm. These pioneers became the foundation upon which the great traditions of the Army Air Corps, the United States Air Force, Naval Aviation, Coast Guard Aviation and Marine Corps Aviation were founded.

◉ Americans at War in the Air In Pictures and Illustrations:

Dr. Edmund Gros, MD, co-founder of the "Lafayette Escadrille"

The Lafayette Escadrille chose very distinctive markings: the red, white and blue to honor the American colors, and the Indian chiefs to uniquely signify American pilots, who couldn't openly identify themselves as Americans

The Lafayette Escadrille initially flew the Nieuport 11, shown above, and nicknamed "Bebe"

The squadron soon shifted to the slightly larger, faster Nieuport 17

The primary opposition was the revolutionary Fokker "Eindecker"

Lafayette Escadrille pilots at Chaudun, July 1917. Standing L-R, Soubiran, Campbell, Parsons, Bridgeman, Dugan, MacMonagle, Lovell, Willis, Jones, Peterson, Maison-Rougle. Seated - Hill, Masson and "Soda", Thaw and "Whiskey", Thenault, Lufbery, Johnson, Bigelow, Rockwell.

Members of the Lafayette Escadrille at Chaudun, France-July, 1917. Included with them are the famous lions "Whiskey" and "Soda"

A 1917 recruiting poster for the new Army Air Service

The American pursuit squadrons flew mostly SPAD's
built and supplied by the French

The only American built plane used in the war was the
DeHaviland DH-4, a two-man observation aircraft

Often forgotten are the observation balloons used by Americans in the war: the Type-R balloon, seen above, was used by all balloon companies

Balloonists had a dangerous job, spotting enemy positions, artillery, and even enemy aircraft, which were often shooting at them

Col. William "Billy" Mitchell, Chief of the Army Air
Service in France

Sergeant-Pilot Norman Prince in his French uniform

The elaborate Norman Prince mausoleum at the National
Cathedral, Washington, DC

Raoul Lufbery poses in his French pilot's uniform, 1917

Lufbery playing with "Whisky"

The wreckage of Maj. Lufbery's plane, May 19th, 1918

Sergeant-Pilot Victor Emmanuel Chapman, the first
American aviator killed in action, 1916

Sergeant-Pilot Kiffin Y. Rockwell, first American to down
an enemy aircraft in combat, May 18th, 1916 but killed in
action September, 23, 1916

The "ace of aces," Capt. "Eddie" Rickenbacker

Before the war "Fast Eddie" Rickenbacker was a
pioneering race car driver

Rickenbacker wearing his Medal of Honor, awarded 1930

Lieutenant Quentin Roosevelt, supply officer, Issoudon, France, 1917

1st Lieut. Quentin Roosevelt, in aviation costume, leaving his machine after a flight..
Photographer: SC. Location: Aviation Field, Issoudon, France.
Date: December 12, 1917. NARA Ref#: 111-SC-80210

Roosevelt, a pilot at last, wearing his Junior Aviator's
wings, early 1918

The graphic photo of Roosevelt's crash site, staged by the Germans to much outrage

Quentin Roosevelt's initial resting place, on the field where he fell

Today, two brothers rest side-by-side in France: Quentin is on the left, and older brother Theodore Roosevelt, Jr., on the right.

Second Lt. Frank Luke, Jr., an "ace" second only to "Eddie" Rickenbacker

Cpl. Eugene J. Bullard wearing aviator's wings, a French Fourragere, and his Croix de Guerre, 1917

2nd Lt. Ernest R. Bleckley

1st Lt. Harold E. Goettler

French troops find the crashed aircraft and retrieve the vital information on the location of the "Lost Battalion"

Us Navy Aviation recruiting poster, 1917

LT. David S. Ingalls, the Navy's first "ace" (and the only Navy ace of the Great War)

Wings of the Great War: Original US Army Aviator (Signal Corps) wings, 1917-top; US Army Aviator wings-1917 (L) and US Navy Aviator wings-1918 (R)

⊙ Americans at War at Sea

The United States Navy was ready to do battle at sea with big guns facing off against the capital ships it expected to have to fight. That was not, however, the war the US Navy would encounter. Instead, the Navy would find itself tasked with long days of arduous convoy duty and harrowing patrols against the enemy's primary maritime threat: the u-boat. This was a war the Navy was largely unprepared to fight, initially, and during the actual months of combat, the Navy's revered battleships and cruisers would criss-cross endless miles of ocean with little to do.

Emulating the so-called "great navies" of that time (Britain, Germany, Japan, Italy, Austria-Hungary), the US Navy had been concentrating on the construction of new classes of battleships and cruisers. Less attention had been given to the role of undersea warfare or effectively thwarting a submarine threat. Likewise, scant attention had been paid by the Navy to transporting troops and protecting convoys, the tasks that proved to be the most pressing naval needs as America entered the war. Almost zero thought and planning had been given to any role for naval aviation except for the one allocated to long-range patrol plane scouting.

As the Navy began wartime operations, it had 207 ships in commission, manned by 65,777 officers and enlisted men. Naval aviation consisted of only 45 qualified pilots, 200 more in training, 54 seaplane-type aircraft, and 1,250 enlisted men stationed at three bases in Massachusetts, on Long Island and in Pensacola, Florida. The submarine service had eighteen commissioned hulls and the Navy could put approximately fifty destroyers to sea (although many more of both classes were authorized under the Big Navy Act of 1916). Troop transports were practically non-existent; but, eighteen former German luxury liners, interned in port at the start of the war, were quickly turned into troop ships.

What the Navy did have, but would find little use for in this conflict, was an aging fleet of 23 coal-burning pre-dreadnaughts, 14 oil-fired modern battleships (in commission or under construction), and 34 cruisers. Another ten battleships plus six ships of an entirely new class called `battlecruisers" were funded and on the construction schedule.

The battleships, as it turned out, had no one to fight. The Royal Navy, the largest naval force in the world, had the German Navy effectively bottled up in the North Sea or tied up pier-side in various Baltic homeports. The Kaiser and his Kreigsmarine admirals were trying to engineer a breakout, but had not quite figured out how to pull it off.

The u-boat force, on the other hand, was quickly bringing the Allies to their knees: There were not enough swift, light cruisers or small, even faster destroyers, to prevent the German submarine force from wreaking havoc against allied shipping. Britain, in particular, was in constant need of re-supply from abroad in order for her to stay in the war. If Germany could deny Britain the supplies she needed, which was clearly happening, it could be a fatal blow.

Royal Navy destroyers were in short supply, and the US Navy had a surplus, based on usage. A handful of these "greyhounds of the sea" could make a difference. Britain was also aware that American ingenuity and skill could crank out new hulls rapidly; in fact, another 200-plus US Navy destroyers were in various stages of design and construction. One American shipyard, at Mare Island, California, completed the *USS Ward* in seventeen days, from keel laying to launching.

The other "raw commodity" that was in demand, after three years of slaughter, was manpower; something else the United States had in abundance. The crucial replacements would need to cross an ocean to get to the front lines; however, and the job of getting them there fell to ocean transport.

The Navy at the Outset of Hostilities:

The Navy had re-built itself in the early years of the 20th Century to pummel its opponents with big guns, and had bred its leadership to operate large fleets at sea in highly choreographed maneuvers. It was going to take some very hard work and wholesale re-thinking to turn the situation around. Fortunately, the US Navy had some senior leaders who would prove equal to the task aided by some daring young commanders who were willing to take their ships "in harm's way."

We have already noted that, from a design and construction standpoint, the Navy was in capable hands: Rear Admiral David W. Taylor, the Chief Constructor of the Navy, was an engineering genius for the ages. In a few short months, and right after his boss, Navy Secretary Daniels, ordered a halt to battleship construction in July, 1917, Taylor was able to swiftly turn the efforts of the shipyards and ironworkers to producing destroyers, sub chasers, and troop transports.

Secretary Daniels was in over his head strategically and theoretically, but he had an able Assistant Secretary who was more than equal to the task: Franklin D. Roosevelt. Young Roosevelt, fifth cousin to the recently retired President "Teddy" Roosevelt, was a dynamo who threw his energies full-throttle into the problem of churning out the proper hulls, recruiting the men necessary, and mobilizing the ships needed to get the hundreds of thousands of troops to France. Franklin Roosevelt spent eight years on the job as Assistant Secretary of the Navy and he has seldom gotten the credit he deserves for the herculean efforts he expended.

One of the ideas that Roosevelt pioneered and shepherded that made an immediate difference was his insistence on placing guns and qualified

Navy gun crews aboard merchant ships. Otherwise defenseless merchantmen could begin to make at least a small difference in protecting themselves. Roosevelt also got behind the idea of the convoy system: merchant ships began sailing in groups protected by a screen of destroyers and light cruisers. The convoy concept was initially belittled by senior Navy leadership as being beneath the Navy's dignity as a fighting force; but, when it proved to be immediately effective, the Admirals quickly changed their minds.

Roosevelt also favored what became known as the "North Sea Mine Barrage." Under this plan, an extensive mine field was laid between the Orkney Islands and Norway in an attempt to keep German u-boats from gaining access to the shipping lanes south of the North Sea. The plan was put into effect in early 1918 with over 100,000 deep and shallow mines in a wide swath across the seaways the u-boats had been using to transit from their home ports to their "hunting grounds." It took a great deal of manpower and resources to get the mines in place—plus some forty million 1918 dollars—but the job got done by July. It remains to speculation how successful the operation might have been given time; but, with only three months remaining in the war, the trap still netted four known u-boat "kills" with another three or four "possible" sinkings. In an ironic twist, the removal of these mines, after the war, proved to be some of the most dangerous duty of the conflict. The Navy was still awarding combat decorations like the Navy

Cross and Silver Star in 1919 to sailors and officers who were engaged in mine sweeping operations after the Armistice.

Admiral William S. Benson sat atop the apex of the leadership pyramid of the US Navy. He was the first-ever Chief of Naval Operations or CNO, and held the post from 1915-1919. He was a graduate of the US Naval Academy, Class of 1877, and spent the greatest part of his career at sea: He was a true "blue water sailor," battleship skipper, and certified member of what was unofficially called the "Big Gun Club." These were the officers who were devoutly dedicated to large caliber cannons afloat. As CNO, he secretly tried to scuttle naval aviation entirely in 1919 but he was quickly and firmly overruled by Assistant Secretary Roosevelt.

Benson was, at least, a very capable administrator. He had to single-handedly define the office of CNO and grapple with the explosive growth of the Navy during the Great War. He firmly believed that the Navy was headed, in future, toward a global maritime leadership role that would require substantial commitments to capital ships, but he was at least willing to recognize the immediate threat and pressed hard for the building of more destroyers and sub chasers to combat the u-boat menace. He was wary of the Royal Navy—as a competitor—but also willing to help them, as allies, to win the war.

When England begged for destroyers from the US Navy, right after America entered the war, Benson sent a small squadron of six relatively new flush deck, "four stack" ships to Queenstown, Ireland, in May, 1917, under the command of CDR. Joseph Taussig. When the ships arrived, after a bruising crossing in severe storms, Taussig was asked by the British admiral commanding at Queenstown when he would be ready to go to sea and fight. Taussig's reply became Navy lore: "We are ready now, sir, or just as soon as we finish refueling."

The arrival of Taussig's little squadron occasioned the creation of a well known painting by the prolific maritime artist Bernard Gribble (1872-1962). Entitled "The Return of the Mayflower" the oil on canvas depicted the small but intrepid line of destroyers chugging into Queenstown, flags flying. It became a favorite of Franklin Roosevelt's and hung prominently in the Oval Office as soon as he occupied that famous space.

Another of the dominant personalities in the Navy as America's war commenced was Rear Admiral William S. Sims (October 15, 1858-September 25, 1936). He, like his boss, Admiral Benson, was an Annapolis graduate, Class of 1880. Sims, from the very outset of his career, made a name—and a reputation—for himself in advocating for the Big Gun but also stressed that those guns should be used, and with regularity. He argued, not convincingly at first, that if the Navy were going to base its strategy on gunnery at sea, then the guns should be exercised, and often: He was aiming to make gunnery practice a cornerstone of preparation for battle. The senior officers above him apparently failed to grasp his logic, even though the theories of Captain Alfred Thayer Mahan and the reforms of Commodore Stephen Luce were beginning to sink in.

Sims didn't get much of anywhere, although he steadily moved up in rank, until he risked his career by writing directly to President Roosevelt about his concerns in 1902. He managed to catch Roosevelt's ear and the President reacted immediately, making Sims the Navy's Inspector General for Gunnery Practice. Sims was then both a rising star and somewhat a thorn in the side of his superiors.

Promoted to Captain, Sims was named to command the battleship USS Nevada, in 1916, after which he was promoted to Rear Admiral and President of the Naval War College (1917). As war became imminent, President Wilson decided to send Sims to London to take on the post of Senior Naval Representative to Great Britain. It was a good choice: Sims was a known admirer of the Royal Navy and had made many friends among the senior officers of that service.

Soon after Sims arrived in England, he developed a very clear idea of what America's Navy would need to do to help her allies: the u-boats and their unrestricted submarine warfare were the clear threats, not the high seas German Fleet. He began arguing vociferously for Admiral Benson and the Wilson Administration to send as many destroyers and small anti-submarine patrol craft as possible, and to do so quickly. Sims also saw the need to immediately gather up allied shipping into convoys and protect the vital ships with escorts.

Benson worried that Sims had fallen under the spell of the Royal Navy and was not seeing the "big picture;" but, when the shocking loss of tonnage began to be reversed dramatically by the convoy system, even Benson came around. Sims was made Commander of all naval forces in Europe, a post he would hold for the balance of the war.

Naval Operations Commence in Earnest:

As the convoy system began to take hold, Sims requested even more destroyers. There was a reluctance on the part of the Navy Department to strip its western defenses (along the East Coast) of these fast, nimble, and useful ships. Nonetheless, eight more were ordered to Queenstown and a second destroyer base was opened at Bantry Bay. Additional resources were made available when the US Coast Guard was added to the mix: By law, upon the declaration of war, tactical command of the entire Coast Guard passed to the Navy Department. In August, six destroyer-like Coast Guard cutters were transferred to Admiral Sims' command in Europe. By the end of that month, 35 destroyer-type ships were operating in and out of Bantry Bay and Queenstown. These ships conducted vital patrol and convoy duties in and around Britain, across the Irish Sea, and well out into the Atlantic.

As the months wore on into early 1918, the need to get American troops and materiel to France quickly made the system of convoying to Ireland and England first before sending supplies across the English Channel undesirable. Admiral Benson pressed to open a port for American destroyers at Brest in the Bay of Biscay, closer to the action. Admiral Sims was not in favor, since Brest did not have the port facilities to handle his precious ships. Benson's view prevailed, however, and a very substantial effort was thrown into building piers, docks, repair facilities, and fuel storage at Brest. This effort finally got into high gear just as the war was ending.

The expansion of operations directly into France also pushed the US Navy further east, into Gibraltar and the Mediterranean. In "The Med" the primary threats were the Austro-Hungarian Navy operating in the vicinity of northern Italy; and, the Ottoman Empire, cruising the eastern Med. Then, of course, there were the dreaded u-boats, who tried hard to interdict shipping coming through the Straits of Gibraltar. To assist the Allies in countering these adversaries the Navy Department assigned a flotilla of craft, under Rear Admiral Albert P. Niblack (1859-1929). The Mediterranean

Squadron consisted of three modern light cruisers, five ancient destroyers, ten converted yachts, a handful of patrol craft and six Coast Guard cutters.

In the far-off Pacific, it was almost as if there was no war, as far as the US Navy was concerned. The colorful, peaceful, and tropical ports of call, such as Pearl Harbor, Manila, and the China Station, remained pretty much at status quo for the duration of the conflict. The only exception, and it was a minor dust-up, occurred just one day after America declared war, and it happened on the sleepy island of Guam; which was a US Territory.

At the beginning of the war, in 1914, the German commerce raider *SMS Cormoran* had been caught in Apra Harbor, Guam, refueling. She was immediately impounded as an "enemy combatant." There she languished, her crew "guests" of the United States, for nearly three years. Upon the declaration of war, the American Governor of Guam demanded the ship's formal surrender. The German captain refused and immediately began preparations to scuttle his ship rather than hand it over. Navy sailors and US Marines attempted to stop the scuttling, firing on the Germans. Nine of the *Cormoran's* crew were killed when the ship blew up and sank. These were the first shots fired by America in the Great War—and they were also the first, last, and only shots fired by US forces in the Pacific.

The first significant action between US Navy and Imperial German Navy units took place on October 15, 1917, off the coast of Ireland. The *USS Cassin* (DD-43), a new 4-piper, flush deck, destroyer spotted the *U-61* and immediately initiated a chase. The *U-61* tried to pull away, but was not anywhere near as fast as the *Cassin*. The submarine executed a quick turn and fired off a single torpedo before reversing course and plunging beneath the waves.

The torpedo, fired close to the surface, "porpoised" several times as it sped toward its target. The *Cassin* tried to maneuver out of the way. Seeing that the torpedo was unerringly headed toward the ship, and was likely to strike the stern where the destroyer's depth charges were armed and ready, Gunner's Mate First Class Osmond Ingram did not hesitate. He raced to the depth charge rack and tried to toss the heavy barrels over the side. Sadly, he was too late and the torpedo slammed into the stern shattering it. The explosion blew off the rudder, triggered the depth charges, and hurled Ingram into the sea. The ship survived, but Ingram did not, becoming the first US Navy enlisted casualty of the war. The *U-61* made good its escape, and the *Cassin* was towed into port for repairs. Ingram would be awarded a posthumous Medal of Honor.

One month later, on November 17th, the destroyers *USS Nicholson* and *USS Fanning* were escorting a convoy south of Ireland when a lookout aboard the *Fanning* spotted a periscope in the water nearby. The *U-58* was lining up a shot on one of the ships in the convoy. Both the *Fanning* and the *Nicholson* raced to the spot where the u-boat had been spotted and dropped a single depth charge each. One or both charges scored, damaging several of the sub's systems. The *U-58* came to the surface, but then started to descend again. The *Fanning* dropped another trio of depth charges over the sub's position, this time knocking out all the ship's electrical power as well as her dive planes. *U-58* was headed to the bottom unless something could be done. Her captain ordered an emergency "blow" of the ballast tanks which popped the ship back to the surface; but, the boat was severely damaged and unable to maneuver.

After an exchange of deck gun shots, one of which, from the *Nicholson*, struck the *U-58*, the u-boat crew threw up their hands and surrendered. The German sailors were evacuated to the *Fanning*, but not before they managed to open the sea cocks on their u-boat. The submarine quickly filled with sea water and sank. Thirty-eight of the forty u-boat crewmen survived and spent the rest of the war as POW's. The skippers of each US destroyer (and the sharp-eyed lookout) were decorated with the Navy Cross. This was the one and only ship-to-ship action of the war wherein the US Navy gained a clear victory.

The *USS Jacob Jones* (DD-61) had just finished escorting a convoy to Brest in early

December, 1917, when she was ordered back to Queenstown for resupply and reassignment. Shortly after she left Brest, On December 6th, she was making for home port and steaming in a zigzag pattern, when she was spotted by the *U-53*. The submarine launched a spread of three or four torpedoes. One of the "fish" was spotted, and the helm was thrown hard over, but it was too late: the torpedo slammed into the stern blowing off the ship's rudder and knocking out all electrical power to the vessel. The destroyer was mortally wounded and started to sink. No distress signal could be sent due to the loss of power, and since she had sailed alone, no ship was nearby to assist.

The ship's skipper, CDR. David W. Bagley (1883-1960), who would later become a Vice Admiral in WW II, knew that the depth charges on the stern had been set to "ready" and would explode as soon as the ship's stern plunged beneath the waves. He ordered an emergency "abandon ship" and got as many of his crew into life rafts as quickly as he could, but the ship sank in eight minutes. The depth charges did, indeed, cook off, and 66 men were killed in the explosions or the aftershocks. There were only 38 survivors.

The only other Navy ship lost in combat conditions during the Great War was the *USS San Diego*, ACR-6, an armored cruiser. *San Diego*, with a complement of 830 officers and men, had been commissioned in 1907. By 1918, she was reaching the mid-point of her intended service life, and she was considered "too old" to be on the "front lines;" therefore, she was assigned to convoy duty in the Western Atlantic.

USS San Diego, and several cruisers like her, were tasked with bringing convoys out of ports along the Atlantic Seaboard and getting them to mid-ocean where the faster, newer, and more agile destroyers from Queensland, Bantry Bay, or Brest would take over and bring the convoys the rest of the way. It was dull, rugged, and generally boring duty for the cruiser crews who schlepped up and down the stormy east coast trying to make sure that noting happened to their merchant charges.

The venerable cruiser had left Portsmouth Naval Shipyard, New Hampshire, on July 18, 1918, headed to New York to pick up a convoy. At 1100 the next day, July 19th, while steaming in a zigzag pattern—as required—near the Fire Island, Long Island Lightship, the *San Diego* was rocked by a powerful explosion. The blast ripped open her hull along the port side. The port engine room was exposed to the sea, and seawater knocked out all power to the ship. Buckled bulkheads prevented critical water-tight doors from being closed and the ship began to fill with water.

The commanding officer, Captain Harley H. Christy, thought his ship had been torpedoed. He immediately got the crew to battle stations and they looked for—and shot at—anything that resembled a periscope. A number of rounds were fired; but, as it turned out, there were no actual periscopes in the area.

Christy quickly ascertained that his ship was mortally wounded. She would not answer the helm and there was no propulsion power available. The captain wanted to drive his wounded vessel up on the beach, which was tantalizingly close to starboard, but it was not possible. Christy efficiently got his men ready to abandon ship. His decisive actions undoubtedly saved many: All but six men got off the ship—a remarkable achievement.

What sank the *San Diego*? To this day, no one is totally sure but the best guess is that it was a sea mine, probably laid by the *U-156*, which was known to have been in the vicinity at the time and laying mines along the Long Island coast. The *San Diego* was the largest US Navy ship lost in the war.

The largest single loss of life for the US Navy occurred when the *USS Cyclops* (AC-4) disappeared in the Atlantic sometime after March 4, 1918. *Cyclops* was a refueling vessel whose routine duties consisted of transferring large amounts of coal (8,000 long tons capacity) from port to port, as needed, for the Navy's coal-burning ships. On her fateful final trip, she had picked up, in Brazil, a cargo of almost 10,000 long tons of manganese ore, used for making munitions, and she was headed to an armaments plant in Baltimore.

The *Cyclops* has been the subject of long-standing sea tales relative to the supernatural forces at work in the Bermuda Triangle, which she did, indeed, transit on her mysterious last voyage. Although no one knows what really happened to her, it is doubtful her loss can be attributed to alien abduction, mystical forces, or giant magnets sucking her to the bottom. What probably happened to her, however, is almost as eerie.

The voyage seemed to be cursed from the outset. *Cyclops*, after seven years of heavy service, was tired: When she left port in Rio, her starboard engine was totally inoperative due to a cracked cylinder. This reduced her to half power before she even sailed. Secondly, she was overloaded: she had taken on 2,000 more tons than her normal capacity probably because manganese ore, which is denser than coal, takes up less space; therefore, more could be stuffed into her holds, even though doing so could have created a dangerous overload condition. Third, her captain, Naval Reserve LCDR George W. Worley, was, by all accounts, a near lunatic.

Worley wasn't even his real name: his true identity was Johan Frederic Wichmann, born in Hanover, Germany, with known sympathies for his native land. It speaks to desperate times and a shortage of qualified sea captains that the Navy somehow certified him and granted him a commission as a Lieutenant Commander in the Naval Auxiliary Reserve. "Worley" had been a ship's master, but of questionable virtue and even more suspicious cargoes, including, it was said, opium. He was also known to have had the personality of a martinet and some of his former crewmen compared him to the notorious Captain Bligh of *HMS Bounty* infamy.

Somewhere in the south Atlantic, this witch's brew of aged equipment, malfunctioning engines, overloaded cargo, and personality disorder ran into a powerful storm. Did her cargo shift? Did she run into a rogue wave? Did she run across a u-boat (post war German records say "no")? Did her corroded beams snap—or did her captain? None of the 306 crew and passengers survived to tell the tale, and her wreckage has never been found.

The second largest loss of life during a single ship action was the fate that befell the *USCGC Tampa* on September 26, 1918. *Tampa* was one of the doughty Coast Guard cutters "drafted" into the Navy in 1917. She had safely escorted a merchant convoy from Gibraltar to Ireland and was headed to port in Wales when, late in the day, she was spotted by *U-91*. The submarine turned, lined up a firing solution, and launched a single torpedo from a stern tube toward the totally unsuspecting cutter. Being only 500 meters away, the shot could hardly have missed, and it didn't, striking squarely amidships. The 190-foot long vessel snapped in two like a twig, throwing a huge fireball into the early night sky. She sank like a stone, taking with her 111 Coast Guardsmen, four Navy personnel and sixteen passengers, none of whom likely had more than a few seconds to consider their fates. It took until Memorial Day, 1999, but all 111 Coastguardsmen of the *Tampa* were posthumously awarded the Purple Heart.

Was the United States bombed by the German Navy in the Great War? Yes, it was; but not much damage was done. On the morning of July 18, 1918, the *U-156*, the same submarine likely to have dispatched the *USS San Diego* with a sea mine, boldly surfaced outside of Orleans, Massachusetts, off Cape Cod, right on Nauset Beach. The commander, Kapitanlieutnant Richard Feldt, ordered his deck gun to open fire. The sub sank a civilian tugboat and all four of its wooden barges before quietly slipping away. It was more of a tail-twisting than a serious attack, but those shells were the first hostile rounds to fall on American soil from a foreign power since Mexico fired on Fort Texas in 1846.

To help close the gap between a lack of destroyers and the u-boat threat, the US Navy ginned up a plan to rapidly manufacture a whole new class of small boats called "sub chasers." The idea was that these essentially throw-away boats, used in vast numbers, would be like hounds against foxes, bringing the quarry to bay until the bigger guns of the destroyers or cruisers could be called on scene for the kill. Most were 70-ton, 110 foot long wooden boats armed with a single 3-inch "pop-gun" and a rack of depth charges. They were powered by one gasoline engine that could drive them along at 20 knots—which was faster than a surfaced u-boat. Sometimes, like the hounds, they would hunt in packs of three or four: once a u-boat was "cornered," three of the sub chasers would stop and drop underwater passive listening devices to detect the u-boat machinery. Bearings would triangulate a position which would be sent to the fourth sub chaser. The attacking sub chaser would race in and drop depth charges. It was a great tactic in theory, and the sub chaser groups claimed up to nineteen u-boat kills during the war; but, none were ever verified.

The sub chasers were too slow and too small to escort convoys; they could not make good headway in rough seas; and, with their gasoline engines, they were floating fire hazards. Over 450 were ordered, and almost 80 found their way to Europe before the war was over. They were put into service, as Admiral Sims said with a sigh, "because we have them." There was one unexpected benefit of their existence, however: Command of these "boats" (some true Navy men disdained to call them "ships") went to a number of junior officers who were up-and-comers. These seagoing skippers, by the time WW II commenced, would take over the helms of the large cruisers, battleships, and aircraft carriers, with excellent experience under their sea caps.

At the outbreak of the war, the US Navy was only beginning to appreciate the value of the submarine. In this regard, the Imperial German Navy was light years ahead. Almost all the Navy submersibles, at the start of the war, were "experimental;" that is, only a handful had been assigned to combat operations. Most were engaged in hydrographic work or the development of submarine tactics. One small force of seven L-Class subs was deployed to Ireland and another four older K-Class subs were sent to the Azores. None of these submersibles had any success against enemy surface ships or u-boats, but a lot of lessons were learned.

The "Big Gun" Navy was not totally sidelined in the war. As a nod to a staunch ally, a US Navy battleship division was invited to join Admiral David Beatty's Grand Fleet of the Royal Navy at Scapa Flow in December, 1917. Rear Admiral Hugh Rodman brought five dreadnaughts to Europe to become the Sixth Battle Squadron of Beatty's fleet: *USS New York*, BB-34 (Rodman's flagship); *USS Delaware*, BB-28; *USS Wyoming*, BB-32; *USS Florida*, BB-30; and, (arriving, February, 1918) *USS Texas*, BB-35. These particular battle wagons were all coal burning, assigned because the Royal Navy had insisted that only coal burning ships be integrated into Beatty's fleet: Britain had plenty of coal, but not enough petroleum.

The Royal Navy didn't really need the extra 14-inch guns the US Navy battleship division sported, but the ships nonetheless served a very useful purpose: Admiral Rodman's ships replaced a like number of aging Royal Navy pre-dreadnaughts, all of which were then laid up. This freed the large crews of these ships to be redistributed to the newer, smaller, light cruisers, destroyers and submarines that were re-populating the fleet. This bait-and-switch did not escape CNO Benson's attention, but he let it ride knowing full well that the deployment of his battleships would be good for US Navy morale, give prestige to the crews, and offer on-the-job training for thousands of his officers and enlisted men. Rodman was also going to be in the forefront of whatever happened in the Grand Fleet, which might give an opportunity to the US Navy to have some say in wartime strategy. All in all, it wasn't a bad trade off.

A second battleship division was sent to England in August, 1918, under Rear Admiral Thomas Rodgers. *USS Nevada*, BB-36, *USS Oklahoma*, BB-37, and *USS Utah*, BB-31, were all oil burners; but, in this case, they brought along their own fleet oiler—and a tug, just in case someone needed a tow. This group was based at Bantry Bay, Ireland, and assigned to escort duty; but, the war would be over within three months of their arrival. As a result, this group saw no significant action; in fact, it only left port once to chase a contact which turned out to be a false alarm.

Rodman's division didn't fare much better. Although they were on station for over a year, they did not fire a single gun in anger. The division took part in several exercises and convoy runs, but the closest any of the ships came to combat was the *USS New York* colliding with a German u-boat on October 14, 1918. No one knows for sure which u-boat was so unlucky as to wander into the path of the lumbering *New York* as she was making for port. It was either the *U-113* or *U-123*, both of which were recorded as lost with all hands, in the vicinity of the *New York* on or around the date of the collision. In any case, the *New York* was punched hard in the starboard side followed, moments later, by a second bump that snapped off one of her two propellers. The *New York* limped into port, and when she was dry-docked for repairs, a huge indent in her hull, shaped like the bow of a u-boat, was discovered. Even though by accident, the *USS New York* was credited with the only "kill" by a US Navy battleship in the Great War.

The grand confrontations at sea between massive fleets bristling with big guns envisioned by the admirals who led the US Navy before the Great War did not happen—nor would they ever happen, not even two decades later in WW II. Instead, the Navy was relegated to thousands of hours of arduous, boring, convoy and escort duty across some of the roughest ocean waters on the planet. The targets they sought were often hidden beneath the waves, not sailing majestically atop them. It was a tough assignment with very little opportunity for glory—or even to fire a gun, for that matter. Yet, it was vital to the protection of the lifelines that sustained the troops on the ground, mostly in France, who were doing the bloodletting necessary to bring the Central Powers to heel. It may not have been glamorous service, but it turned out to be essential—and it set the stage for an entire re-thinking of what the US Navy would—and could—be used for, something that would prove very valuable as the world churned ahead to another vast conflagration only twenty-one years further down the sea lanes of history.

⊙ Americans at War at Sea In Pictures and Illustrations:

US Navy destroyers on convoy duty towing a manned observation balloon

Adm. William S. Benson, the Navy's first CNO, 1915-1919

"The Return of the Mayflower"

The German commerce raider *SMS Cormoran*, sunk in Apra Harbor, Guam, April 7, 1917

USS Cassin, DD-43

Photo # NH 458-KN GM1 O. K. Ingram, USN, on board USS Cassin (DD-43), 15 October 1917

Gunner's Mate Ingram attempts to save the *USS Cassin* from its own depth charges, October 15, 1917. Ingram would be killed but his bravery would be rewarded with the Medal of Honor.

313

U-boats in Kiel, 1917: *U-61* may be the second ship
outboard

USS Fanning, DD-37

USS Nicholson, DD-52

Crew of the *U-58* surrendering, November 17, 1917

USS Jacob Jones, DD-61, sinking after being torpedoed
by *U-53* December, 6, 1917

The *USS Jacob Jones* survivors

USS San Diego, ACR-6

A painting of the wreck of the *USS San Diego* off Long
Island, July 19, 1918

USS Cyclops, AC-4

Reserve LCDR G. W. Worley—in reality: Johann F. Wichmann

The sinking of *USCGC Tampa* by *U-91*, September 26, 1918

A Great War sub chaser

Adm. Hugh Rodman

USS New York, BB-34, in New York Harbor, 1915

⦿ 1918: "The Yanks Are Here…"

January to April, 1918: As the last year of the Great War dawned, the Allies had little reason to be optimistic, though hopes were still high. 1917 had been a crushing year for the British and the French, with appalling loses all across the board, and no great victories to show for all the blood and treasure expended. The French, the common soldiers, the celebrated "Poilous," were in open revolt: division after division had told their officers they would no longer make futile advances on the enemy's works. Henceforward, they would only participate in defending the lines they had established already. The British Prime Minister, David Lloyd George, restricted the numbers of replacements being sent to France to purposefully slow down his thick-headed commander, Sir Douglas Haig, who never hesitated to throw more troops at the enemy in vast waves. The Allies were exhausted and dispirited by their experiences; yet, there was hope: The Americans had finally arrived and everyone was waiting for them to catch up and pitch in.

The Americans were streaming into France in vast numbers. General Pershing had four full divisions by January, but only one, the 1st, was remotely ready to go into action—and they had been training for six months. Not knowing, of course, that the war would last only eleven more months, Pershing was holding back, anticipating a massive contribution to the war in early 1919.

Meanwhile, pressure was ratcheting up to squeeze Pershing's timetable drastically: Allied manpower reserves were all but depleted. Conversely, America had plenty of manpower, but Pershing remained adamant about waiting until he felt his troops were ready, and he was stubbornly opposed to allowing his troops to be amalgamated into the decimated ranks of his allies. With the generals at loggerheads, the politicians stepped in—again.

Lloyd George made a direct appeal to President Wilson via Colonel House. Secretary Baker was drawn into the discussion as well, but both Baker and the President agreed they should leave the decision up to Pershing. With the argument then at full circle, it ended. Pershing would not budge and that was that. Pershing was not simply being bull-headed: he had good intelligence, gathered by some of his best staff officers, that indicated the Germans were not as strong as they looked: they were not the unstoppable juggernaut the British and the French thought them to be. Although the Central Powers had effectively knocked Italy out of the war, and the Russians had collapsed in revolution, the German people were starving and the economy was on the verge of collapse. Even having three fronts reduced to one—the Western—and dozens more divisions available, the makeup of the freed divisions was not robust. The Central Powers had also suffered grave losses in men and materiel in 1917. Pershing believed—and he would be proven right—that the French and British, as bad off as they complained of being, would be able to hold on and hold off the Germans until Pershing and his men were ready.

Contemporary records clearly indicate that General Pershing was occupied in early 1918 as much with spirited debates over the deployment of his troops as he was engaged in effectively training and placing those troops where they needed to be. Discussions over "amalgamation" waxed and waned from January through April and Pershing must have become heartily sick of all the pushing and shoving, but to his immense and everlasting credit, he never gave in. He did bend a few times, but he never broke. In an effort to buy time and promote some harmony, Pershing made a few agreements, here and there, for positioning small groups of battalions and regiments with French or British forces, but always as complete units, and always under their own officers. In one memorable exchange, an exasperated General Foch fired at Pershing with: "You are willing to risk our being driven back to the Loire (which would be far to the southwest and way beyond Paris)?" Pershing shot back an emphatic, "Yes, I am willing to take the risk. Moreover, the time may come when the American Army will have to stand the brunt of this war, and it is not wise to fritter away our resources..." In April, however, the tempo and deployments began to change.

Late April, 1918: Knowing he was not going to win the amalgamation argument with Pershing, Foch got the best deal he could: he agreed to begin folding complete American units into so-called "quiet" sectors of the French lines near St. Mihiel. This substitution would free up experienced French divisions to bolster other more active sectors. So it was that on April 20, American ground forces got into the war in a meaningful, but not very satisfying way, near the village of Seicheprey.

Major General Clarence Edward's 26th Yankee Division (so called because it was made up of units from New England) held ground all along the St. Mihiel line from April through June. On April 20, the Germans began a "box bombardment" against the 102nd Infantry, and its positions in and near the village of Seicheprey. This type of barrage concentrated artillery in a "box" around an enemy strong point and while the troops were busy avoiding the falling shells, a "storm troop" attack would be positioned to overwhelm the shocked and battered troops as soon as the artillery was lifted. The barrage lasted a horrifying 36 hours during which time the "boxes" were magnified, isolating one American unit from another. Once the barrage lifted, the German storm troopers pounced. Two companies of infantry and a machine gun unit were overrun. Before a counterattack could be organized, the Germans were gone, having inflicted 80 killed, 424 wounded, and 130 valuable prisoners taken. The Germans left behind 150 dead and 450 wounded, but it was still a complete and shocking embarrassment to the Division and Pershing was beside himself. It was an inauspicious start, and it did not help improve relations between Edwards and Pershing, who personally despised each other. Better days were coming, however, and they would begin with a significant American victory at Cantigny one month later.

<u>May 28, Cantigny:</u> The bloodied and embarrassed Yankee Division relieved the 1st Division at St. Mihiel and the 1st moved north to the Montdidier sector near Amiens. The commander of the 1st, Major General Robert L. Bullard, was an "old tiger," a Regular army officer with a West Point pedigree who had seen service in the Spanish-American War, the Philippine Wars, and the Mexican Border Conflict. He was aggressive and ready to fight. The "Big Red One" was posted to a sector run by a French commander, and as soon as Bullard got on scene he was actively seeking a combat assignment. He was anxious to prove his men were up to the task and to avenge, in a sense, the first impression left by Maj. Gen Edwards's men at Seicheprey (Bullard, too, had a passionate hatred for Edwards). The French commander was hesitant to oblige, so he bumped the request up to Marshall Petain himself. Petain was more than happy to see what Bullard's men could do, so he directed his subordinate general to permit the 1st to attack the village of Cantigny.

Cantigny sat at the apex of a salient created by the defending Germans that pushed into the

Amiens sector. The French had attacked twice before, gained the village, but were subsequently repulsed both times by spirited German counter attacks. The 28th Regiment, commanded by Col. Hanson Ely, drew the assignment to capture Cantigny.

Using a rolling barrage of artillery, Ely's troops, numbering about 3,500, stormed the village at 0645. Cantigny was captured with surprising ease, and minimal casualties, but the eager Americans soon discovered, as had the French, that holding the town was a lot harder. The first German counteroffensive materialized at 0830, but was repulsed. For the remainder of the day, the Americans had to endure an intense German artillery barrage designed to dispirit and dislodge the Yanks. It did not work; so, at 1710 the Germans launched another counterattack, much larger and more intense than the first.

This second attack was thwarted when the 1st Battalion, 26th Infantry, commanded by Major Theodore Roosevelt, Jr., was thrown into the line. A third assault was attempted at 1810, but it, too, was turned back. The Americans began to push out from the village and consolidated their positions, making a salient of their own over a mile beyond the town.

The Americans held, and over the next two days it became apparent to the Germans that the doughty Doughboys were not going to be dislodged, even though it would cost them 1603 casualties, including 300 killed in action. Among those lost was Pvt. Matthew B. Juan, the first Native American and first Arizonan to be killed in the Great War.

Cantigny was the first large scale American action of the war and proved to the French that American arms could be counted on and trusted to hold up their end of any bargain.

June and July: Chateau-Thierry, Belleau Wood, and the Second Battle of the Marne: The full weight of the Central Powers remaining forces, which were considerable, began to concentrate on the Allied lines northeast of Paris during late May. The German High Command knew they were in a race against time: they needed to make substantial inroads against the Allies and attain key objectives quickly, before the poverty, economic collapse, and dwindling supplies of materiel they faced at home crippled their abilities to carry on the fight. Given the shaky fortunes of both the British and French, and the lack of Americans in the front lines, it seemed to be a decent gamble.

The Germans pushed hard and by May 27, they had driven the French back to the Marne, within fifty miles of Paris. General Foch and Marshall Petain desperately needed troops and began plucking reserves from other sectors. The American 1st Division stretched its lines to allow several French divisions to pull away and race toward the Marne. The next two American divisions that Pershing considered nearly ready were the 2nd and 3rd. He reluctantly ordered them forward and placed them under the overall command of the French.

Elements of the 3rd Division, commanded by Maj. Gen. Joseph T. Dickman, a West Point graduate and veteran of four wars prior to the Great War, arrived first. The 3rd Division's 7th Machine Gun Battalion leapt off their trucks on May 31st and went straight into action along the Marne assisting the French in holding onto the main bridge across the river. Dickman's infantry arrived on June 1st and immediately stretched out across an eight mile sector, which it would tenaciously hold onto for the next month.

The 2nd Division, commanded by Maj. Gen. Omar Bundy, yet another West Pointer and veteran of the Spanish-American War, the Philippines, and Mexico, arrived in the Chateau-Thierry sector on June 1st. The 2nd had an interesting organization: of its two main brigades, the 3rd was Regular Army, and the 4th consisted solely of US Marines. The Marines, of course, wanted to get "into the fight," but their pre-war and early war numbers were not large enough to warrant a division of their own; thus, they were incorporated into an Army division (although they fought under their own Corps officers and during the course of the war the entire division was twice commanded by a Marine Corps general).

Chateau-Thierry: The spirited German drive toward Paris halted on the Paris-Metz highway just short of the Marne River at the end of May. It was not, however, the end of their efforts to proceed. Re-gathering their strength, the Germans made a lunge toward the bridges over the Marne on June 1st. The French 10th Colonial Division and elements of the American 2nd Division were there to stop them—and they did. These Allied forces went even further, and pressed forward a counter attack on June 3 and 4. This drive pushed the Germans away from the river and kept all the bridges and crossings in the hands of the Allies. After this action, it was the Marines turn to show what they could do.

Belleau Wood: The Germans remained thickly invested in a deeply wooded enclave near the Marne called the Bois de Belleau; or, in English, Belleau Wood. Maj. Gen. Bundy assigned his Marines, under the command of Pershing's respected former Chief of Staff, Brig. Gen. James Harbord, US Army, to take the woods. Thus began a bloody, intense, horrific fight that lasted from June 3 to June 26 and would result in the worst casualties ever suffered by the fabled US Marines in any single battle (a record that would last until the Battle of Tarawa in WW II).

The Germans began the dance by flowing out of the woods with a broad, sweeping, fixed-bayonet charge across waist high fields of wheat. The Marines were told to hold their fire, which they did, until the Germans were only one hundred yards away. When the rifle fire and machine guns let loose, the Germans were scythed down as if they were the sheaves of grain upon which they trod. Hundreds died before the survivors beat a hasty retreat back into the forest.

The initiative was handed off to the 5th Marines. The French forces, "repositioning" to the rear, shouted to the Americans to fall back and consolidate. Capt. Lloyd W. Williams of the 2nd Battalion retorted with his now famous words, "Retreat? Hell, we just got here!" The Virginia Tech graduate did not retreat. He charged, with his men, across the blood-stained wheat, and was mowed down as quickly as his enemies. Posthumously promoted to Major and awarded the Silver Star, Williams Hall at Virginia Tech was erected in his honor after the war.

The next Marine attack on the woods began in the late afternoon of June 6th. The 3rd Battalion of the 5th Marines and the 3rd Battalion of the 6th Marines stepped off in good order, in perfect lines, and waded into the same wheat fields so recently sanctified by their compatriots and their enemies. Sadly, they met pretty much the same fate and were gunned down in droves.

Another legendary line was uttered by a brave Marine that day, this time by Gunnery Sergeant Dan Daly. As the men of his 73rd Machine Gun Company strode into the amber waves of grain he shouted, "For Christ's sake men, come on! Do you want to live forever?" Daly had experience in this business of war, having already earned not one, but two Medals of Honor: one for his China service in the Boxer Rebellion in 1900 and a second for bravery in Haiti in 1915. He was one of only nineteen men to have ever received the Medal of Honor twice, and only one of two who had awards in different wars.[5] Unlike many of his men, Daly survived the slaughter of that day, and would receive both an Army Distinguished Service Medal and a Navy Cross for his actions at Belleau Wood.

In the meantime, across the way, out of the wheat fields and up what was dubbed Hill 142, another group of Marines was slogging to the summit. Once atop the knoll, the Germans wasted no time in trying to shove the Marines back down. Gunnery Sergeant Ernest A. Janson of the 49th Company, 5th Regiment, looked around and found that every officer in his outfit was either dead or wounded. It would be up to him to rally the remaining men and consolidate their victory—or lead them back down the hill in retreat. He decided they would stay. As the men began to dig in, Janson spotted twelve German soldiers racing to the top of the knoll with a collection of five light machine guns. Janson shouted a warning, then charged. He killed the two leading Germans with his bayonet and chased the rest, who dropped their

---

[5] After 1918, the rules were changed and only one Medal of Honor could thereafter be awarded to any individual.

weapons and ran. Janson was seriously wounded in the altercation, but survived to become the first Marine to be decorated with the Medal of Honor for the Great War.

Despite the staggering losses, the Marines pushed on. The 3rd of the 6th finally made it into the woods only to run into more machine guns, barbed wire and snipers. The fighting became hand to hand. Virtually every officer-thirty-one in all-was down, along with another 1,056 enlisted casualties: It would be the Marine Corps' worst day ever. They were, however, in the woods, and they would be there to stay.

Attacks and counter-attacks raged back and forth over the next several days. On June 9th, a joint French-American artillery barrage of ferocious intensity reduced much of the woods to kindling; however, the broken trees and utter devastation actually made it more difficult to clear the forest.

The Germans threw the bulk of five divisions at the Marines over the course of the battle, with terrifyingly bad results. One German battalion at the forefront started the fight with 1,200 men. After they withdrew, the battalion mustered 120—a casualty rate of 90%. The Americans suffered almost as badly: the Army and Marines tallied 9,777 casualties including 1,811 killed in action. No reliable figures on German totals were ever produced, but estimates number over ten thousand, including 1,600 prisoners.

It was at Belleau Wood that another Marine Corps legend was born: that of the "Devil Dog." Reportedly, German dispatches from the front, back to central headquarters described the Marines as "Dogs from Hell;" or, in German, "Teufel Hunden." The nickname stuck.

Post battle, the 5th and 6th Marine Regiments were awarded the French Fourragere for their bravery (an award comparable to the Presidential Unit Citation in the American military). A light aircraft carrier was named for the battle in WW II and the modern Navy commissioned a large amphibious helicopter carrier with the same name.

Over the decades since the battle, historians and tacticians have debated the wisdom of throwing long, straight lines of unflinching Marines across those deadly wheat fields, then pushing them into the macabre cyclone of hell in the woods. None, however, have ever questioned the bravery of those who could later claim, "I fought at Belleau Wood."

<u>July 15: "The Rock of the Marne:"</u> The 2nd Division had done their duty at Chateau-Thierry, Belleau Wood, and then captured the key town of Vaux. Next, it was the 3rd Division's time of trial by fire. To the northwest, the Germans had launched yet another desperate offensive at the French. The French lines bent, but they didn't break. The Germans did get across the Marne in some areas by as much as five miles, however. With the French

pushed back, the Americans of the 3rd Division had to stretch their lines even further to stay in contact with their allies and prevent a flanking movement on their left.

General Dickman, who had been rotating two regiments to the front and holding two in reserve, was forced to put all four regiments up on the line. On July 5, his men and their resolve would be put to a strenuous test. The Germans attacked all along Dickman's reed-thin front, but the blows fell most heavily on the 30th and 38th Infantry Regiments.

The 30th was commanded by Col. Edmund L. "Billy" Butts, West Point Class of 1890, and a more stubborn, determined warrior the Germans could not have faced that day.

The 38th Infantry was commanded by Col. Ulysses Grant McAlexander, another West pointer, Class of 1887. Born in 1864 and named in honor of the man of that hour, McAlexander would also prove to be a tough and stalwart opponent for the Kaiser's vaunted storm troopers.

The German High Command had decreed this offensive would be the crowning glory of their drive to open the roads straight to Paris and a swift conclusion to the war. This would be the so-called "Friedensturm," the "push for peace," and it would be Col. Butts and Col. McAlexander and their men who would be at the point of the German spear.

The Germans began the day with a rolling barrage from 89 field artillery pieces that lasted four thumping hours. As soon as the guns stopped crashing, a full division of shock troops was thrown at the American lines. The Yanks took a terrible pounding, but slowly began to give back worse than they were getting. Interlocking fields of machine gun fire mowed down the Germans in droves and stopped them before they could consolidate any positions across the Marne. One German regiment sent 1,700 men into the maelstrom. At the end of the day only 150 were left standing.

Butts' men were forced back before the end of the day's fighting, suffering grievous casualties, but they held. McAlexander was less fortunate, initially; but he, too, made a courageous stand.

Without warning, the French division on McAlexander's right turned and fled. The right flank of the 38th was totally exposed. Like Chamberlain at Gettysburg, McAlexander simply "refused his right;" that is, he bent the right hand portion of his line back, at an oblique angle, to defend his flank. Meanwhile, the German's punched a hole in his front. McAlexander pulled companies away from the left to shore up his center. At one point during the day, the 38th was fighting on three sides. The men dug deep into their reserves of both bullets and valor, and doggedly shoved the Germans back. By nightfall, the worst of the fighting was over and the Germans had failed, skedaddling back across the river.

The gallant stand of the 30th was impressive, but the intrepid fighting of the 38th inspired General Pershing to describe the action as "one of the most brilliant pages in our military annals." It also earned McAlexander and the 38th the sobriquet of "The Rock of the Marne." Both colonels would attain promotion to general officer and each would be decorated with a Croix de Guerre and a Distinguished Service Cross.

July-August, 1918: By the end of July, 1918, Gen. Pershing had one million Americans in France, with many more on the way. Again, all of this preparation and training was aiming for the big push to close out the war, which Pershing felt would not come until 1919, at the earliest. Almost no-one on Pershing's staff—not even Pershing himself—would have predicted that the end of the war was less than four months away.

With so many men at hand, it was time to organize them into corps structures with multiple divisions. Once the various corps were organized and staffed, they, in turn, would be grouped into separate armies. The American First Army was established on August 10th.

Feeling it was finally time to test the capabilities of his forces on a large scale, Pershing went to his new friend, Marshall Petain, seeking an opportunity. He already knew what he wanted to attempt—the reduction of the large German salient into the Allied lines at St. Mihiel—but he'd need French cooperation to make the attempt. Petain and Pershing went to newly-promoted Marshall Foch and made their case. Foch agreed to the enterprise with one caveat: once the Americans had successfully reduced the salient, they would pivot north and help the French drive into the Meuse-Argonne region. Pershing consented.

September 12-14, St. Mihiel: In September, 1914, the German Army had punched a hole into the Allied lines between the Meuse and Moselle Rivers that had given them a two-hundred square mile, arrowhead-shaped salient. The Germans had stubbornly held onto their advantage for almost four years. Recently, the Germans had decided to retreat from the salient, which would free up a number of their divisions and help shore up their hard-pressed lines further to the north. Pershing and his Allies did not know this, of course; so, with a degree of irony, they determined to finally clear the salient, and actually commenced their attacks several days before the Germans had intended to pull out anyway. Although the Germans were somewhat prepared for the movement, and had issued some orders organizing the pull-back, they were nonetheless surprised when the Americans pounced on them from two sides with great ferocity. Here is how the battle progressed, from start to finish:

Not wanting to tip-off the Germans, Pershing had originally determined to begin the battle with little to no artillery bombardment. This thinking was very much in line with Pershing's disdain for "fixed" or trench warfare: He had come into the European theater convinced that the Americans, to be successful, would have to employ more "open field" operations, sweeping across large areas of territory. His opinions had been somewhat validated by operations earlier in the summer at Chateau Thierry and Belleau Wood, even though those actions had tallied larger than expected casualty lists.

Lengthy artillery bombardments might do some good in softening up the lines immediately in front of an attack, Pershing knew, but they also gave the enemy plenty of time to figure out where the attack was coming from, and offered him the opportunity to reposition troops from other areas to blunt the push. In any event, Pershing's staff was successful in convincing him to soften up the lines with at least some artillery effort. The Americans, after all, had 3,000 guns available, mostly French, and some use might as well be made of them. The guns opened up for seven hours along the western edge of the "arrowhead" and for four hours along the southern flank. The dual-front pounding would give the Germans pause, so Pershing's staff reasoned, so as to make them wonder where the real attack was going to come.

In addition to the massive amount of artillery deployed, Pershing also had 1,400 aircraft and nearly 300 tanks at hand. Many of the aircraft (about 700) were flown by Americans under the command of Col. Billy Mitchell. The rest were an amalgamation of French, British and Italian squadrons. The American tanks were under the command of the resourceful but impetuous Lt. Col. George S. Patton.

Morale and esprit de corps among the Americans was sky-high, but the weather refused to cooperate: What started as a fast-moving offensive soon began to bog down under un-relenting rain and stultifying mud. The Americans, attempting a pincer movement and hoping to trap thousands of retreating Germans between two fronts, gamely pressed ahead.

The Germans, who had already started to pack up, in anticipation of pulling out of the salient, had their artillery way out of position; therefore, the French and Americans had little to worry about from the German guns. On the other hand, with some preparations already underway, many German divisions were able to hurry out of the salient in good order thereby frustrating the American plan to "bag them up." Nonetheless, by battle's end, some 15,000 Germans were prisoners of war, and that was not an insignificant number.

Colonel Patton's tanks made their presence known and proved, during the course of the two-day battle, that tanks had a role to play and could be of significant strategic value. These early machines were clumsy and balky, and many of them bogged down in the grasping muck, but others were able to grind forward and under Patton's inspiring leadership took out one machine gun nest or artillery battery after another.

Mitchell's bombers and attack aircraft also played a key role, when the weather permitted, harassing Germany's retreating troops from the air and preventing counter-strikes by German air assets. The Germans abandoned vast amounts of stores and artillery all along the roads they travelled, mostly because of constant harassment from above.

The St. Mihiel salient was cleared in two days, despite the bad weather and the opposition. The battle validated several important points, not the least of which was that Pershing and his division commanders were capable of large scale, combined operations. The Americans suffered 7,000 casualties, which was regrettable; but, with over a half-million men actively engaged, the numbers could have been far worse.

September 26-November 11, the Meuse-Argonne Offensive: The forty-seven days between the commencement of the Meuse-Argonne Offensive and the Armistice would be the most exhilarating and also the most grueling days of the war for the AEF. Those weeks would begin with a dead-stop ordered by Marshall Petain as soon as the Doughboys cleared the St. Mihiel Salient.

The hard-charging Yanks, hot on the heels of the retreating Germans, were poised to take the city of Metz. Petain, however, wanted Pershing to swing northwest, as he had promised, toward the Argonne Region, and join the all-out offensive the Allies were about to commence. This drive was intended to smash the Hindenburg Line for good and push the Central Powers all the way back inside Germany by Christmas. The British, further to the north and west, and the French had pulled together every conceivable remaining resource for this attempt to seal the fate of Germany. Britain's Marshall Haig, and both French Marshalls Petain and Foch, believed that with their reorganized forces and the heft of the growing American Armies, the four-year stalemate could finally be ended.

The first, and certainly one of the most difficult tasks, was going to be the logistics involved in re-staging the 600,000 American troops near St. Mihiel. That job fell to a young staff colonel in the First Army by the name of George C. Marshall. After having graduated from VMI in 1901, and service as a company commander in the Philippines, Marshall rose rapidly in the Army and by 1917 was a major. Wartime service saw him vaulted to full colonel in the National (not Regular) Army by August, 1918.

His brilliant mind and keen eye for logistics were put to good use in the Meuse-Argonne re-alignment challenge. In ten days he managed to relocate all the troops, 3,000 artillery pieces, and 40,000 tons of supplies using only three available roads. This minor miracle was also done under the cover of darkness, to keep the massive movement from German eyes.

By September 26th, just twelve days after the St. Mihiel operation, the Americans were in position to jump off. They could not have had a more formidable challenge. Their front would be some fifteen to twenty miles wide. On their eastern flank would be the wild and swiftly flowing Meuse River. On the left flank was the densely wooded Argonne Forest. Both flanks offered the Germans the advantage of the high ground. Straight ahead of the Yanks was a landscape of rugged copses, lateral ridges, and a defensive position fifteen miles deep, slathered in barbed wire and bristling with machine gun nests set up with interlocking fields of fire. The German artillery could fire down on the Americans from both sides. It was not possible to go around or flank the enemy: the Americans would just have to push ahead and do the best they could under daunting circumstances. Marshall Petain privately expressed misgivings, thinking the Americans would do well if they got to the second of the three German defensive lines by the end of the year. Pershing was convinced the weight of his numbers would have an immediate effect, backed, as they were, by nearly 3,000 artillery pieces, almost 200 tanks, and eight hundred aircraft. Initially, his optimism would be rewarded.

Before the entire battle played out, it would involve over one million American troops and at least a half million German soldiers. It would be the largest, bloodiest, costliest operation in US military history (until WW II). It would be the biggest battle of the war. It would also produce the war's most famous stories of valor under fire and make enduring legends of a few.

On the first day of battle, the enormous waves of Americans in their over-sized divisions rolled over the first two lines of German defenses with ease, but also at significant cost. The massive numbers of Yanks were just too powerful, even for the strongest German positions and the thickest fields of barbed wire. The next day, however, things began to slow.

Once again, heavy rains deluged the battlefields for two days straight, bogging down nearly all the tanks that weren't already knocked out of action. The horrible weather also hampered the progress of the mud-caked artillery caissons and grounded all the aircraft that could have been put into play. The Germans took advantage of the situation by rushing additional infantry divisions onto the fields at key pressure points.

Experience—or lack thereof—began to tell: the veteran American divisions buckled down and pressed ahead. The new divisions, especially the less than fully trained National Guard battalions, struggled and floundered. The advance became ragged and came to a complete halt in certain sectors. Coordination fell apart altogether between some units. As September came to an end, it was clear to Pershing that he would have to call a general halt to operations and reorganize, which he did.

The second phase of the battle began during the first days of October. Pershing was able to rotate out several of his less experienced divisions and replace them with veteran units. The offensive began to lurch ahead again. A key objective was clearing the Argonne Forest, for which much effort would be expended. It was during these crowded days that one of the most compelling incidents of the war took place: It concerned the plight of the so-called "Lost Battalion."

The 77th Division, one of the first divisions to France, was a rugged crowd made up of Yanks from in and around New York City. These "Metropolitan Men" were brawlers from the Bronx, street wise kids from Brooklyn, and stock brokers from Manhattan, all tossed into one blender and served up to the Germans as a cocktail of "tough guys" with attitude. They would not disappoint. On October 2nd, six companies of the 77th's 308th Infantry Regiment, along with one company from the 307th, and two machine gun companies from the 306th were under the command of a bespectacled, Harvard-educated, Wall Street lawyer by the name of Major Charles Whittlesey. His executive officer was Captain George McMurtry, another Harvard man, and a playboy stockbroker who, in his younger days, had stormed San Juan Hill in Cuba with Col. "Teddy" Roosevelt. The machine gun companies were led by a plucky California National Guard captain by the name of Nelson Holderman.

Whittlesey had been given orders to secure an old mill, road juncture, and railroad crossing inside the Argonne Forest. His objective was part of a general advance undertaken by the 77th and a division of French troops. The 77th jumped off in good order but regiments lost contact with one another as soon as they stormed into the thickly wooded forest. The French, for reasons never determined, abandoned the attack altogether and withdrew from the field leaving the Americans with an open flank and facing serious repercussions from the Germans. The commander of the 77th, disgusted with his French allies, was forced to order a retreat to consolidate his lines.

Whittlesey's group had charged so far ahead that they did not receive the order to fall back. The Germans immediately recognized Whittlesey's predicament and fell in behind his positions. In short order, the 554 men accompanying the major were surrounded and cut off. Whittlesey was forced to dig in on a hillside and wait for help. The Germans closed in and began blasting away.

Whittlesey's only means of communication with his commander was a cage full of carrier pigeons trained to dash "home" with rolled-up messages tucked in capsules banded to their legs. He released one after another of his precious birds only to see them shot from the sky by expert German marksmen. Finally, one of the brave birds made it through.

In the message Whittlesey sent, he logged what he thought his position might be and he requested artillery support. To this day, no one knows whether Whittlesey wrote down the wrong coordinates or if the artillerists cranked in the incorrect numbers, but shells soon started to fall— directly on top of Whittlesey's men. Several soldiers were killed before Whittlesey managed to launch his last pigeon with a desperate plea: "Our artillery is dropping a barrage directly on us. For heaven's sake stop it."

Whittlesey and his dwindling command managed to hold out for six terrifying days before being rescued. During that time they hurled back every German attack made against them, ran out of food and water, stripped bandages from the dead to use on the living, robbed corpses of their unexpended ammunition, and fought the enemy hand-to-hand. Whittlesey ignored every German plea to surrender. The "Lost Battalion" was only found after some amazing heroics performed by two intrepid aviators, Lieutenants Goettler and Bleckley, who paid for their bravery with their lives—as chronicled in the previous chapter, "Americans At War In The Air."

Whittlesey, McMurtry, and Holderman were all wounded, but all three would survive, and be decorated with the Medal of Honor. Whittlesey was promoted to Lieutenant Colonel on the spot. Of the 554 men who went into the Argonne with him, only 194 made it out alive, almost all of them wounded. Of the remaining men, 197 were killed and 163 were tallied as missing in action or taken prisoner. Seven men, in total, would be decorated with the Medal of Honor for this action with another twenty-eight receiving the Distinguished Service Cross.

On the very same day that the "Lost Battalion" was finally being rescued, a 31-year old Acting Sergeant of the 82nd Infantry Division was fighting in the same deep woods several miles to the west. His unit was under heavy fire from a protected machine gun position. Alvin York was told to take a patrol, try to outflank the machine gun, then take it out. As York and his men worked their way around to the gun, they walked into a German battalion headquarters, surprising the officers and men stationed there. Everyone of the Germans threw up their hands in surrender. The men on the machine gun, however, did not, and they immediately concentrated their fire on York and his men, wounding a number of them. As calmly as could be, the intrepid Tennessee sharpshooter dropped to one knee and began to pick off the German gunners, one by one. He killed twenty of them before they, too, surrendered. York and the remaining men of his patrol bandaged up their wounded then marched 132 German prisoners back to their shocked commander's headquarters. Sergeant York would also be awarded the Medal of Honor for his actions on that day.

At the end of October, the Americans had cleared the third and final German line of defenses and swept the Argonne Forest of the opposition. The First Army, which had borne the brunt of the fighting, was nearly spent, however. Pershing also realized that he was taking too much of his personal time directing the action in this sector, to the disadvantage of managing the strategy of the entire theater of operations. He decided to relinquish control of First Army to Lieut. Gen. Hunter Liggett. Pershing also saw that the First Army had grown unwieldy at nearly a million men; so, he established the Second Army and placed Lieut. Gen. Robert L. Bullard in command. Both Liggett and Bullard were "old hands" and West Point graduates whom Pershing had known for many years—and trusted.

Liggett was quick to grasp that his new command was in need of some rest and regrouping. At the expense of a few precious days of action, he pulled many of the units off the line, got them replacements, hot food, new uniforms, more ammunition and some of the new Browning Automatic Rifles that were coming into the inventory. He insisted that infantry and artillery commanders work more cooperatively. He had his engineers repair the roads his men would need to press ahead. He even procured hundreds of fresh draft animals: The Army still needed horses and mules by the thousands, despite its growing mechanized focus, to pull the guns and supply wagons.

When Liggett's rejuvenated divisions were ready to attack on November 1st, they moved ahead so far and so fast they literally ran off the maps their commanders were using to track their progress. By the 8th of November, Liggett's Army was at the Meuse River and the Germans were on the ropes.

The Meuse-Argonne offensive was nearing its end, but it been a costly fight: 26,277 Americans had been killed, and another 95,786 were wounded. The next move would be up to the Germans, and it would come surprisingly swiftly.

The Armistice: "The 11th hour of the 11th day of the 11th month..." At the end of September, as the Americans were about to rout the German Army in the Meuse-Argonne, the German High Command in Berlin quietly, secretly, and firmly told Kaiser Wilhelm II and Chancellor von Hertling that the military situation was unequivocally hopeless. General Erich Ludendorff, head of the Army, said he could not even guarantee holding onto the front for another twenty-four hours.

These sobering revelations lead to a swift series of political changes in Germany over the next six weeks. Surrender was unthinkable and out of the question; but, an armistice to conclude the fighting until a peace treaty could be negotiated would be acceptable, if agreeable terms could be obtained. President Wilson was proposing just that, an armistice, based upon his so-called "Fourteen Points." Not even Wilson's Allies were sold on these points; however, much less the German government. Some aspects of the terms became a framework for discussions but there was still much to consider. A key sticking point for the Germans at this early stage of negotiation was the Allies insistence on the Kaiser's abdication. Germany was unwilling to consider "such a monstrous possibility."

Events out of Berlin's control soon intervened, however. German troops in the field were all too aware that the war was lost. Entire divisions lobbied to lay down their arms and go home. They were too proud to refuse to fight, but they were no longer willing to die for nothing. During the evening of October 29th, the Imperial German Navy revolted at their base in Wilhelmshaven: no German u-boats or other warships would put to sea. A war-weary and starving populace soon joined the sailors and the revolution spread across Germany in days.

On November 9th, a new German coalition government took control and the Kaiser abdicated and fled to Holland. A German peace delegation was already heading to meet with Marshall Foch aboard his private train in the forest of Compiegne. Representative officers from all the Allied Forces met with the German negotiators, and an armistice was hurriedly agreed to, one which would take effect at eleven in the morning, Paris time, on the eleventh day of the eleventh month. Only after the Armistice took effect, would peace talks begin, but for all intents and purposes, the war was over.

It was not soon enough, sadly, for American Private Henry N. J. Gunther, of Baltimore, Maryland, 313th Infantry Regiment, 79th Division. At 10:59 AM on the morning of November 11th, 1918, he foolishly charged a German machine gun roadblock near Meuse. The German soldiers, knowing the Armistice would go into effect in just one minute, tried to wave Gunther off. Gunther's own companions tried to dissuade him, but he would not relent. His mates related afterward that Gunther had told them he wanted one last chance for redemption before the war ended. Gunther had recently been a sergeant; but, he had been demoted after censors discovered disparaging remarks about the army and the war that he had tried to send home. He wanted his sergeant's stripes back.

Gunther kept running at the Germans, and when he fired off a shot the gunners finally had no choice: they fired back, killing him instantly. Private Gunther was the last of 53,402 American battle deaths during the Great War. Ironically, he was the grandson of German immigrants who had emigrated to the United States to seek a better life.

◉ <u>1918: "The Yanks Are Here..."in</u> <u>Pictures and Illustrations:</u>

Doughboys marching to the front

"Over There"—Finally...

Cantigny, May 28th, the first test: the 1st Division goes "Over the Top"...

...and secures the village on the first day, after heavy fighting

Major General Robert Lee Bullard, Commander, the 1st Division: "The Big Red One"

Col. Hanson Ely (center, right) with his 28th Infantry staff

BRIGADIER GENERAL FRANK A. PARKER, LIEUTENANT COLONEL THEODORE ROOSEVELT, AND MRS. ROOSEVELT AT ROMAGNE

Lt. Col. Theodore Roosevelt, Jr., (center) who served
valiantly in the Great War

Major General Joseph T. Dickman, Commander, 3rd
Division, first soldiers to the Marne

Major General Omar Bundy, Commander, 2nd Division, early 1918

Brig. Gen. James Harbord (C), Pershing's first Chief-of-Staff commanded the 2nd Division's US Marines at Belleau Wood

Capt. Lloyd W. Williams, Commanding Officer, 51st Co., 2nd Battalion, 5th Marines: "Retreat Hell! We just got here!"

Sgt. Maj. Daniel Daly wearing both of his Medals of Honor: "For Christ sake, men! Do you want to live forever?"

Gunnery Sgt. Ernest A. Janson, first US Marine awarded
a Medal of Honor in the Great War

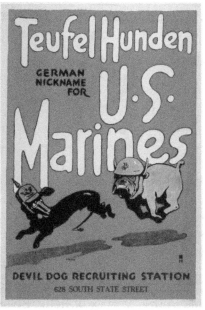

USMC "Devil Dogs" recruiting poster, 1918

French lithograph of the fighting in Belleau Wood

US Marines in the "vortex of hell," Belleau Wood

The 3rd Division becomes "The Rock of the Marne"

38th Infantry seal commemorating their Great War valor

Lt. Col. George S. Patton and one of his Great War tanks

An American tank goes into action

Col. George C. Marshall, logistical genius of the Meuse-
Argonne Offensive

The forbidding Argonne Forest in 1918-site of the plight
of "The Lost Battalion"

Lt. Col. Charles W. Whittlesey, Commander, "The Lost Battalion"

Capt. George G. McMurtry
CO/2nd Bn/308th Inf.

Major George McMurtry

Capt. Nelson Holderman

The brave carrier pigeon that got the message through
to stop the artillery

Survivors of 'The Lost Battalion"

Sgt. Alvin C. York, Medal of Honor, the Great War

The Armistice ending The Great War was signed in a
simple train car

Celebrations of the Armistice broke out all over America,
like this one in Chicago

...and in New York City

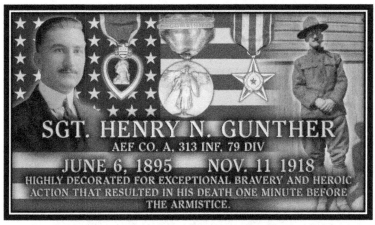

SGT. HENRY N. GUNTHER
AEF CO. A, 313 INF. 79 DIV
JUNE 6, 1895 — NOV. 11 1918
HIGHLY DECORATED FOR EXCEPTIONAL BRAVERY AND HEROIC
ACTION THAT RESULTED IN HIS DEATH ONE MINUTE BEFORE
THE ARMISTICE.

The Armistice did not help Henry Gunther, the last American killed in the war. He died one minute before the cease fire took place.

⊙ 1919: The Legacy of War

It all ended so swiftly. It was certainly no secret to Pershing and his senior commanders that the Central Powers were nearing the end of their endurance in November, 1918; but, the speed at which the capitulation came took many by surprise. Even after the grinding but successful Meuse-Argonne offensive, Pershing remained convinced that he and his two million-man army were aiming toward ultimate victory sometime in 1919, maybe even 1920. Then again, the Allies, and certainly Pershing, were envisioning a complete crushing of the enemy followed by a formal surrender—not an armistice.

The armistice, in a sense, let the Central Powers, Germany in particular, off the hook. Hostilities ceased, which was a relief for all affected by the war, but there was no surrender. The armistice was a pause, a breather, a cushion, between the end of the fighting and the negotiation of a peace treaty. The German economy was in shambles, and the populace starving, but there would be no complete capitulation. The German armies were exhausted, but they walked away with their pride and their weapons. [Note: There would be three extensions of the Armistice before a final peace, the Treaty of Versailles, was ratified and signed on January 10th, 1920.]

The AEF saw 200 days of fighting in the combat theaters they entered. It was one of the shortest stretches of warfare operations in the history of American arms; yet, the intensity of the campaign created, on average, 1,600 casualties a day: 53,402 were killed in combat, 204,002 were wounded, and another 63,306 died of disease or non-combat related injuries or accidents. The grand total was: 320,710; or, about 7.1% of all the forces sent overseas.

Of the four million men (and approximately 35,000 women) who served in the American Armed Forces during the Great War, a little more than half of the men—2.2 million—and a handful of women (less than 10,000) served in France and other posts overseas (Italy, Siberia, Serbia, Poland, and the Middle East). After the Armistice, the flood tide of Americans had to be reversed. Generally, this was done fairly quickly, but it is a little known fact that thousands of Yanks stayed behind. General Pershing established the Third Army, under Maj. Gen. Joseph Dickman, as an occupying force to be left in place, mostly in the German Rhineland.

The AEF, in fact, was tasked with providing about one-third of the Armistice and peace treaty troops required to keep "the watch on the Rhine." Nine veteran divisions of about 205,000 troops in total were left behind after the end of the war. They stayed in Germany until January 24th, 1923, when the American occupation officially ended.

What to do with the tens of thousands of sick and wounded Yanks? The general medical plan was that any Doughboy who could be effectively treated for wounds or illness and returned to duty in under six months would be retained for medical treatment in France. Those requiring longer term care would be shipped home to the States. Special trains to transport these men to new or contract hospitals were provided by the railroad companies. The ports of New York and Newport News, Virginia, were designated as the debarkation terminals for the long-term sick and seriously wounded.

Eventually, almost 150,000 veterans would be cared for as post-war casualties. The most common categories for treatment were: medical (diseases and the after effects of gunshot wounds), surgical, and orthopedic. Special hospitals handled head injuries, amputations (with rehabilitation and prostheses), and the poorly understood area generally described as "shell shock." Mental issues constituted about five percent of all long term casualties among American troops from the Great War. The neuroses these men suffered were no less real than the physical wounds carried by some of their comrades, but it took many years for medical doctors and psychiatrists to grapple effectively with what we now call PTSD; or, post traumatic stress disorder.

Fortunately for the veterans of the Great War, enormous advances in battlefield medicine had occurred since the last large scale American conflict—the Civil War. For example, thanks to inoculations, the typhus and typhoid fever that had killed over 60,000 men in the Civil War caused fewer than 250 deaths in the Great War. Wounds that almost always resulted in automatic amputation in the Civil War were diminished substantially. Injuries that caused horrifying disfigurement, especially to the facial area, could be treated with techniques pioneered by Great War doctors who developed new methods of reconstructive surgery as a result of the conflict. Lung and burn ailments, many caused by exposure to chemical agents and toxic battlefield gases, became better understood and new treatments were developed.

Millions of veterans needed to be re-integrated into society and the workplace. The federal government had no effective programs in place to handle veteran's issues on the scale it faced. The old GAR; or, Grand Army of the Republic, had been the principal champion of veterans rights, pensions, and benefits for the past fifty years, but the aging Civil War veterans were on their way into the history books by the time the Great War ended.

A new champion was needed. The American Legion was born just four months after the Armistice was signed and within one year nearly twenty percent of all Great War veterans were members. No less an icon and hero of the Great War than Lt. Col. Theodore Roosevelt, Jr., was the principal founder of the Legion, with backing by General Pershing.

The Legion quickly became the prime mover in veteran's affairs and it successfully lobbied for passage of pioneering veteran's legislation. The Sweet Act of 1921 created the federal Veteran's Bureau, the predecessor to the Veterans Administration. The new Bureau was to have jurisdiction over veteran's health services, insurance, pensions, and vocational education. The Bureau got off to a rocky start, however: its first director stole millions of federal dollars before being caught and sent to jail. It finally found solid footing under its next Director, retired Brigadier General Frank Hines.

American industry, which had been slow to get organized for war, eventually went into overdrive. When the war ended so quickly, industrial production, which was then at its peak, needed to find new outlets. It soon did, rushing America into the "Roaring Twenties" and the boom times before the Great Depression. Demand for everything skyrocketed, especially automobiles, household goods, and an entire array of new appliances and convenience devices, many of which had come out of wartime innovation and necessity. Here are just a few examples: sanitary wipes; paper tissues; sun lamps; blood banks; tea bags; the wrist watch; zippers; stainless steel; mobile x-ray machines; and—interestingly—feminine sanitary napkins. The "war gods" also got new "toys" including: the tank; flame-throwers; poison gas; tracer bullets; depth charges; hydrophones (for underwater listening); drones; aircraft carriers; and, air traffic control (which was, of course, adapted to excellent civilian usage).

Also left over, sadly, were the seeds of the next world war. This assertion, of course, has been debated for generations, and arguments can be made pro and con. We do know this: The Treaty of Versailles ended up being a bitter and contentious document that satisfied very few. The American Congress, ultimately, blocked its ratification and separate treaties, ending hostilities between the various former Central Powers and the United States, had to be negotiated one by one.

The root causes of the war, as President Wilson saw them, were never properly addressed. He outlined his thoughts in his famous Fourteen Points which he presented personally to his allied partners, at Versailles, in 1919. They were soundly rejected. The core of his proposals concerned self-determination for every nation (read: "democracy"); free trade; freeing colonies for self government; and, a proposal for a League of Nations (the predecessor to the United Nations).

Britain, which had suffered horrible casualties but little territorial damage was worried about coming down on Germany too hard. Britain had age-old ties and Germany had been an important trading partner prior to the war. Britain hoped to restore previously beneficial connections under a new and more democratic German government. France, on the other hand, which had suffered enormous devastation and the worst casualties of any allied nation, wanted to crush Germany, an age old enemy, for good. France wanted territorial concessions, a buffer zone, and above all reparations—or repayment—for the staggering costs of the war.

Germany was stripped of most of her valuable colonies and forced to abandon a significant portion of her armed forces. Fortifications had to be torn down in some areas, and Germany was banned from the international arms trade. The new government had to immediately pay $5 billion in solid gold, commodities, and securities. The eventual amount of reparations paid (by 1932) came to a little over $33 billion dollars, which was a staggering sum in its day.

It could have been much worse. What the Allies required, in fact, did not cripple Germany as badly as many had wished. Germany was left with a core navy and a much smaller but dedicated army. At the bottom line, the German people were left with much to complain about, in terms of their perceived harsh treatment by the Allies, but not so much as would actually prevent them from recovery.

Revenge for the "Fatherland" and pay-back for loss of pride and prestige in the world community became the primary rallying cries for the National Socialist Party—the Nazis. Hostilities may have been suspended in 1918, but they were never ended. The flames of Germany's unrealized ambitions were never extinguished completely and the world would come to realize that error in just one generation.

America, as a nation, came out of the war with great prestige and new respect in the world community. It became clear to the old guard in Europe, and the rising international powers like Japan, Soviet Russia, and China, that America was finally a main character on the world's stage. The Yanks did not win the war by force of arms, but they proved they could fight and fight well. Their very presence, growing by division strength nearly every day, finally convinced the Central Powers they were vanquished. The United States became the international power that many had expected it would become.

Fortunately for America, the twenty-year span between world-wide conflicts would bring to the forefront, at just the right time, thousands of men who had been forged by the fires of the Great War. The junior officers who had fought on the front lines in France or jockeyed destroyers at sea were, by 1940, commanding regiments, battalions, battleships, or aircraft carriers. The colonels and senior navy captains of 1918 were, by Pearl Harbor, general officers or admirals leading divisions or battle groups. The best planner of them all became Chief of Staff of the Army (Marshall). The crucible of the Great War produced Eisenhower, Patton, McArthur, Bradley, Clark and

Ted Roosevelt, Jr. The great admirals of the era like King, Nimitz, Fletcher, Mitscher, Halsey, Spruance, Sherman, and McCain all came from the same experiences. The legacy of one war bled directly into the next. Only in the maelstrom of World War II would the issues that had sent two million Doughboys to France finally be resolved.

⊙ 1919: The Legacy of War in

Pictures and Illustrations:

German soldiers react to the news of the Armistice

German POW's

The American 64th Infantry Regiment celebrating the
Armistice

Doughboys returning home on the *SS Agamemnon*,
Hoboken, NJ-1919

90th Division Victory Parade, Dallas, TX

Battlefield treatment for a wounded soldier

Wounded Great War veterans at Walter Reed Hospital,
Washington, DC

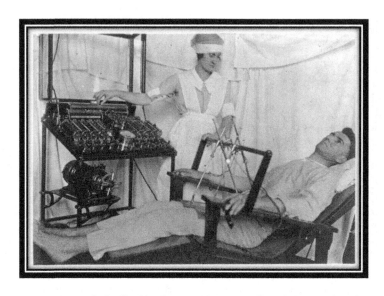

A victim of shell shock receiving early electro-shock therapy

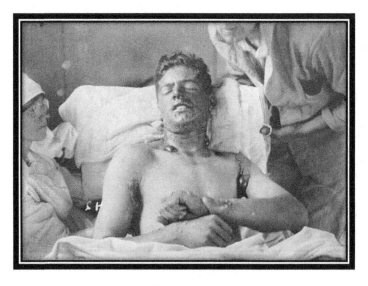

A Great War veteran being treated for mustard gas exposure

The American Legion was founded immediately after the Armistice

One of the very first American Legion Parades, Los Angeles, Memorial Day, 1920

Air traffic control was developed in the Great War
At first, planes were moved across a map as they
reported by radio

The aircraft carrier was invented in WW I: the *USS
Lexington*, CV-2, above, begun in 1921

The Versailles Treaty was signed in the great Hall of Mirrors, Versailles, France, 1921

But did it sow the seeds for the next war?

Acknowledgements: I wish to thank my very special and wonderful partner, Laura Lyons for her constant support, on all levels, as well as her valuable insights and suggestions as this book came together. So, too, I wish to thank my incredibly talented son, Pierce Rosen-Keith, for his technical expertise and his terrific cover design.

Special end note for Educators: Teachers interested in using this book as a module on the history of World War I may contact Peconic Bay Publishing to receive discounted print copies. Every educator who purchases a copy of "America and the Great War" is entitled to a free PowerPoint presentation by sending an email directly to Peconic Bay Publishing at: PBPublishing@optonline.net. Please state your name, school, location, and grade level for our records.

Additional Historical Non-Fiction Books by the Author:

Blackhorse Riders, A Desperate Last Stand, an Extraordinary Rescue Mission, and the Vietnam Battle America Forgot; St. Martin's Press, 2012

Fire Base Illingworth, An Epic True Story of Remarkable Courage Against Staggering Odds; St. Martin's Press, 2014

Crimson Valor, Harvard Alumni and the Medal of Honor; Peconic Bay Publishing, 2011

Stay the Rising Sun, The True Story of USS Lexington, Her Valiant Crew, and Changing the Course of World War II; Zenith Press, 2015

All Blood Runs Red, the Legendary Life of Eugene Bullard--Boxer, Pilot, Soldier, Spy; Hanover Square Press, (coming November, 2019)

Author's Website:

amazon.com/author/philkeith

About the Author: Phil Keith, a native of Springfield, Massachusetts, holds a degree in history from Harvard and has done master's work at Long Island University and the Naval War College. After graduating from Harvard, Phil went directly into the Navy and became an aviator. During three tours in Vietnam, he served with distinction and was awarded, among other decorations, the Purple Heart, Air Medal, Presidential Unit Citation, and the Navy Commendation Medal.

After his wartime service, Phil rose to the rank of Commander in the Naval Reserve and is also a licensed US Coast Guard Master's Mate. As a business executive, he worked for two Fortune 500 firms and is a former assistant professor of business at Long Island University and adjunct instructor at the Rhode Island School of Design, teaching marketing and writing courses.

Phil serves on the planning board for the Town of Southampton, New York, and is a member of VFW Post 5350, American Legion Post 924, Disabled American Veterans, and Vietnam Veterans of America.

He lives in Southampton with his partner Laura Lyons and son Pierce.

Made in the USA
Middletown, DE
22 June 2019